Teaching

Using the Principles of *The Art of War* to Teach Composition

The Way

STEVEN T. NELSON

Ten|16
PRESS
www.ten16press.com - Waukesha, WI

Teaching the Way:
Using the Principles of *The Art of War* to Teach Composition
Copyrighted © 2021 Steven T. Nelson
ISBN 9781645382782
First Edition

Teaching the Way:
Using the Principles of *The Art of War* to Teach Composition
by Steven T. Nelson
teaching-the-way.com

For information, please contact:

Ten|16
PRESS

www.ten16press.com
Waukesha, WI

Editor: Margaret Dwyer
Cover designer: Kaeley Dunteman

For all my students, teachers, and colleagues—
I've learned so much from all of you.

TEACHING THE WAY

Using the Principles of
The Art of War
to Teach Composition

Introduction

Who would've guessed that you, yes *you*, composition instructor, would hold the fate of so many lives in your hands? Whether you are new to teaching or have been working for years, you are engaged in an undertaking with important moral, intellectual, and civic ramifications. Because just like writing is not like anything else in human experience, teaching writing is not like teaching anything else. And your guidance and leadership are going to be crucial to your students' development as writers, thinkers, and human beings. In college they will have many teachers, but you are not like the rest. Because writing is The Way: to knowledge, wisdom, truth, and freedom. It is The Way to much of what's important in life, and whether you know it or not, you are a general in the army of The Way.

This book is designed with two general aims: First, to help you show your students The Way, that is, to appreciate the value of writing, which will improve their writing, thereby improving their lives, preparing them to succeed in the world and make it better. The second goal is to help you develop an effective teaching style that focuses on what's important for composition students and generates energy for both you and your students in ways that will make your time spent more efficient, effective, enjoyable, and satisfying.

Writing: The Way

What do I mean when I say writing is The Way? That's a good question, and I'm not surprised you asked it—you're a composition instructor, after all, with that mix of curiosity, generosity, and intellectual acuity that is allowing you to lead humanity forward to its best possible future. Finally, someone *gets me*, you might be thinking. Yes, I do. But let's get back to writing, the process of writing, which I believe is the way forward in life, the set of skills everyone needs. I mean, can you think of anything more important in life than writing? Not if you think of it as the most advanced, precise, expansive, and expressive form of not only communication, but thinking. Writing is the essence of thinking, just as thinking is the essence of writing, and though we can talk, sing, dance, pray, kiss, hug, make music, program computers, climb mountains, and lots more, writing is the only way to really *say* something, to really *know* anything, to really *understand.* Writing can be the path to knowledge, understanding, enlightenment, independence, freedom, and more.

Conversely, the inability to write and think for one's self can leave a person ignorant and helpless. People who can't think for themselves risk becoming prisoners—to circumstance, the whims of the world, or, in some cases, the selfish intentions of others. One could argue that there are things more important than writing—food, shelter, and clothing. Maybe friendship, health, or love. If you believe in writing, your list may go a little further, but not much. Of course, poor writers, or "inexperienced" writers (some of your students, for example), might say that writing doesn't matter—that it's *just* one method of communication, whose importance is declining. But you know this is not true—that speaking and casual rumination are relatively sloppy, and that to have command of one's thoughts, to understand thoughts and emotions, other people, and the world at large, one must have command of the language.

Now it's true that we spend most of our lives *not writing.* Even dedicated writers may spend only a few hours a day actually writing—pen to paper or fingers on the keyboard—but one's ability to think clearly during all hours of the day, to comprehend what others say and do, discover and understand one's thoughts and emotions, is borne out of an understanding of how to use language, and that knowledge can only come with the study and practice of writing.

Of course, I'm not saying writing doesn't have its limits: sometimes knowing the truth doesn't make it better, sometimes words can't accurately capture thoughts and emotions. Awareness of the ineffable is one of the essential human experiences, but I only understand this because of my ability to use language, to conceptualize this undeniable truth, that some things can't be understood or expressed. I know this because I write.

My History as a Teacher

At this point, you might believe in the value of writing but not in me. Don't worry, I won't take that personally. I see it as a healthy skepticism, your critical mind in action. But be aware that I have spent a lot of time thinking about the student-teacher relationship since I stepped in front of my first class over twenty-five years ago:

- having just graduated with my master's degree in Creative Writing,
- expecting a New York literary agent to contact me any day with the news that not only was I being taken on as a client, but that my novel had already been accepted by a big publisher (I'm still waiting for this call),
- not only having never taught a class, but never having any training in *how* to teach, and not ever having taken a college composition class myself,
- having not paid any attention to how teachers I'd had taught their classes (assuming they just showed up and things just happened, naturally, inevitably, which is how it seemed for lots of them, which I at one point realized meant they were very good teachers),
- having met with the dean of this college only a day earlier, a cold, sunny January Sunday afternoon, at his house (evidence of how desperate they were to find someone to teach the class) when he handed me the textbook (a composition textbook—I'd

never read one before) and a syllabus and told me, "You'll do great, you know what you're doing." Of course, I agreed with him. "Yes, I know what I'm doing" (though really I had no idea what I was doing).

I can still remember the feeling of myself perspiring as I stepped in front of the class on a Monday evening, can still picture the room, even the faces of some of the students that night. I remember the disembodied state I was in as I introduced myself and heard myself speaking, watching myself, wondering how I'd gotten there, imagining what these strangers were thinking about me (none of it good).

I don't remember much more about that particular class, and I didn't think too much about the student-teacher relationship that semester. I was honestly too traumatized by the act of teaching that class to think about how good or bad of a job I was doing or what my students were thinking about me. To honestly think about it at the time would've been too painful.

Somehow I made it through the semester, and then, finally released from what I was then considering to be my punishment for going to grad school, I looked back and, while I knew I didn't do a great job, I told myself I could have done worse, that it had gotten better as the weeks rolled by, and that my students had improved in their writing. I even vaguely remember a student or two thanking me at the end of the semester and saying they enjoyed the class and had improved. Whether or not those sentiments were genuine or not, I don't know. But after that semester, I told myself I could do better. I knew I could do better, that my students deserved better, and I'd be happier if I could make this happen. I don't remember specifically what I changed for the next class I taught, or the one after, or the one after that, but I know that I was improving. But every semester I told myself the same thing—that I could still do even better.

And somewhere along the line, I realized the key to getting better was not just providing better content. While that was important—better readings, better assignments, better instructions—these factors were all always changing for me. Because after that first semester, I taught wherever I could: composition, literature, creative writing, speech classes, business writing, at six or seven schools over the years, any place within driving distance, sometimes three schools in the same semester, two classes at each. So the content was always changing, even for composition classes, each school had its own plan, sometimes a specific textbook, assignments, curriculum, protocols.

But what I was realizing was that the key to me becoming a better teacher was getting the students more motivated to do the work, to care enough to do the best they could. I thought that was a good goal and that if I taught the class well, they'd keep going without me and eventually see the value in doing their best work always, saying what they needed to say, making every word count. Over the years, I paid close attention to motivation. What got students motivated (and what didn't)? What did my motivated students have in common (that the others didn't have)? What could I do to get more students motivated?

To get all my students motivated? These have become the questions I ask myself every semester. Yes, the content and reading and assignments are important, but I now create these based partly on these other questions—how can I get my students to care? To want to do the work?

At some point, I realized my teaching career will always be a work-in-progress and that there will never be an end to me trying to do it better. I've also come to think of the thousands of students I've taught over the years as my most important teachers. I've also learned a lot from my colleagues. I've read books about teaching. At this point, I've spent over half my life trying to get better at teaching, and with this book, I want to share what I have learned with you, my fellow teachers. I want to make your jobs and your lives better. I also want to help you make your students better writers and make their lives better. I wrote this book for them too, all the students taking composition classes. Because writing matters so much.

Sun Tzu and *The Art Of War*

Okay, so what does this all have to do with *The Art of War?* Another good question. If you have already read that book, the connection between Sun Tzu's philosophy and teaching may already be clear. But if you are unfamiliar with this work, and don't have time to read it anytime soon, let me give a brief introduction (and you don't need to read that book to appreciate this one, though I do suggest you put it on your list of books to read at some point).

First off, the title can be misleading as *The Art of War* does not instruct one how to destroy things, but rather how to build them up. The principles of *The Art of War* can show us as teachers how the right kind of strength, sound strategies, the proper attitude, and genuine preparedness can help us earn victories while preserving ourselves.

Historical accounts seem to agree that Sun Tzu was a military general in China who lived around 500 BC. He was apparently a bit of a hermit, but his reputation still reached King Ho-lu, who was in need of military advice (it was a rough time in China—lots of fighting). Sun Tzu was called before the king to explain his strategies about warfare. When he did, the king was impressed with Sun Tzu's philosophies, but also said something like, "That all sounds good in theory, but how do I know it will work?" To prove his ideas were valid, and could be applied universally, Sun Tzu supposedly transformed 180 "court women" into trained soldiers in a single session. How did he do it? We don't know for sure. One story is that he had one resistant "soldier" beheaded to get the attention of the rest. While that can't be confirmed, I'm sure it would've been effective. What we do know is that as a general, Sun Tzu employed his strategic principles to lead troops to a number of impressive victories, allowing the king to take control of supposedly more powerful states. After these conquests, everyone in the know in China knew about Sun Tzu.

In the 2,500 years since, Sun Tzu's ideas on strategy have reached a wider audience—first in China, then other nearby countries, before being introduced to European audiences in the eighteenth century. *The Art of War*'s popularity in the U.S. supposedly started with a 1963 translation by retired U.S. Marine general Samuel Griffith, who applied Sun Tzu's ideas, as other military leaders before him had, to warfare. But it's not so much a book about warfare, destruction, or violence as it is about strategy and human nature, leadership and morality, and directing the energy of the universe where one needs it to go. It teaches leaders how to avoid confrontation, to control situations and *win without fighting*.

Sun Tzu makes this clear when he says, "To gain a hundred victories in a hundred battles is not the highest excellence; to subjugate the enemy's army without doing battle is the highest of excellence." And that's the point of my book—I'm aiming to show you how to teach those hundred students of yours to learn to write without having to fight them, by making them active participants in the process, by making them *want* to learn to write.

I doubt Sun Tzu would be happy with the way *The Art of War* has been used in recent years. There are best-selling books using the principles of *The Art of War* for Business (i.e. how to grab market share from competitors), Marketing (how to get people to want stuff they don't need), and Sales (how to get people to buy stuff, and then more stuff, and then convince them they need even more). There's also *The Art of War for Dating: Master Sun Tzu's Techniques to Win over Women* (the book jacket says, "Where Sun Tzu taught his men how to win wars . . . teaches you how to get laid.") Something of a companion piece, *Sun Tzu for Women: The Art of War for Winning in Business*, promises to show readers how to "trump male colleagues every time."

Reading over this list of titles, it may seem that any hack could churn out a book relating his or her ideas to those of Sun Tzu. So how is this book different? Well, what do all these other books have in common? They instruct readers how to use Sun Tzu's knowledge and insight into human motivation for selfish purposes, to take advantage of others: do this and get what *you* want. But this book, this book you are reading right now, is different from those. True, it may help make your job easier and your life better, two things on everyone's to-do list, but these results will only come about because they are natural consequences of being a better teacher and improving the lives of students. This book, like Sun Tzu's, is about building things up, making things better, not taking advantage of anyone for personal gain. And with the ideas and strategies I am going to share, we composition instructors can reclaim Sun Tzu's principles for moral purposes—for the benefit of our students, and the greater good!

When did I first read *The Art of War*? I'm not sure. I know I was aware of it before I read it, though I can't remember what led me to reading the book the first time. I expected to like it, as I'd always felt myself compatible with Eastern thought from as far back as seeing *The Karate Kid* for the first time. I got it, it made sense. I liked Bruce Lee's idea of "the less effort, the more power." I liked the Bodhidharma quote "All know the way, few actually walk it." Or Ram Dass's, "The quieter you become, the more you can hear." These ideas just hit me as inarguably true. Before reading *The Art of War*, I had read a lot of books on or about Eastern thought and philosophy, and some of them became, even as I was reading them, some of my favorite books of all time. I read *Zen in the Art of Archery* and I said, "Yes!" I read *The Dharma Bums* and I said, "Yes!" I read *Siddhartha* and I said, "Yes!"

I loved them all but never studied the philosophy too seriously, satisfied enough with my understanding and feeling attuned with what they had in common. I know there are differences among Taoism, Buddhism, Confucianism, et cetera, but they all kind of blend together in my mind, with no hierarchy. I've got no favorites. I just pick and choose my favorite parts of each to help me understand myself, others, and the world.

But *The Art of War* was not like any of these books. It was not a story like I was used to reading. Instead it provided insight and practical advice in short, little phrases. The philosophy Sun Tzu was prescribing fit with my desire to be efficient, surprising, underestimated. For example, as a runner, often when I entered a race I wanted to be the one in the back of the lead pack after halfway with everyone asking, "Who is this guy? How does he feel? What is he thinking?" In most races, I liked to sit back just a bit, see the others make a show of leading, fighting for the lead, then, having exhausted their energy stores too soon, come up and pass them when it mattered, before the finish. In pickup basketball games, I'd never show off in warm-ups. I mean, I'd show I was good enough to get picked and play in the game, but no more. Then once the game began, I'd be surprisingly good and effective, much better than the player assigned to guard me, giving my team an advantage they hadn't been counting on. In graduate school, I wanted to be the one who sat back rather quietly and modestly but then dazzled everyone with my work. I wanted people to say to me, "I wasn't expecting *that*." Did this happen? I don't know. If so, surely less than I had hoped. But more importantly, why did I want to be this way? Why do I still? I don't know the answer to that either. To avoid pressure? Maybe. But as Alan Watts, another of my favorite Buddhist writers, said, "Trying to define yourself is like trying to bite your own teeth."

As I read *The Art of War*, the idea for this book came to me. What Sun Tzu was explaining was in a lot of ways what I was already doing in my teaching. When I sat down to start writing this book, my goal was to understand it all better—Sun Tzu, my teaching, my students. I knew if I wrote about it, I'd learn about it. And it's true. I do now understand Sun Tzu's philosophy better. I also understand why I had adopted certain teaching strategies and avoided others. I have become more aware of my strengths and weaknesses as a teacher. And all this happened because the act of writing is The Way, as I have already explained.

One thing I discovered through both teaching and working on this book is that, as I have already said, teaching writing is not like teaching other things. A writing class is different for students, and our roles as teachers are different too. And while some may argue with Sun Tzu's claim that there is a moral purpose to warfare, it's difficult to argue that there is not a moral purpose to teaching writing. And by this I don't mean your students are necessarily writing about morality, ethics, religion, or politics. They may be, but no matter what they are writing about, they are always aiming for the truth, for accuracy partnered with reason. To discover and express it the best way they can. That's what I mean when I say composition class has a moral component embedded into it.

Now you may not have thought you were embarking on a moral mission when you were hired to teach composition. *I'm a writer,* you might think, or *a scholar,* or *critic.* And though that may be true and you may be an outstanding writer, scholar, or critic, you're more than that because you're also a composition instructor—which means it is your duty to meet with the unenlightened and help them. What you teach your students will have a direct bearing on every part of their existence for the rest of their lives.

That may seem like an overstatement, but Sun Tzu says, "A general is the safeguard of the nation" and "guardian of people's lives." That is how you need to see yourself because after your class, your students will be back out in the world—to other classes, with other teachers (many less enlightened than you)—and forced to deal with complicated life situations. They will meet with opportunists, politicians, scam artists, and the like. Even if most of the people they come in contact with for the rest of their lives have good hearts and good intentions, to make it through their lives, to do their parts in making the world a better place, your students need to be able to think for themselves, think critically, understand what they hear and read, and communicate effectively.

This all sounds great, you may be thinking, but I just want to make it through the semester. I understand where you are coming from. That's always my goal too. But there are different ways to get there. You can just put in the time, feed students some basics, correct their mistakes, teach them to churn out "acceptable" work, believe they don't care and that it doesn't matter. It is possible to "survive" the semester this way then get back to what "really matters." I know teachers who have endured long, miserable semesters and even long, miserable careers working like this. If you have read this far into the book, I doubt you are one of them and that you are more likely already a good, if not a great, teacher. And this means you are open-minded, willing to learn, and not opposed to new strategies that will make your classes even more interesting and meaningful for both you and your students. No matter where you are starting from, you can do more. You can do better. You can help your students *and* improve and fulfill yourself. Still don't believe me? That's fine. You shouldn't. You should only believe it when it happens for you.

For the rest of the book, I will present quotes from *The Art of War* (I'm using the Thomas Huynh translation). My goal is to present them in ways that make sense to you and can be applied to your teaching. Like good ideas, sometimes they will appear in quick succession and close to each other, at other times there will be long gaps in between. I hope I have filled in these gaps with some of my own good ideas on ways to make your teaching easier and more effective.

You: The Benevolent Leader

Was it Sun Tzu who said, "With great power comes great responsibility?" No, I think that was Uncle Ben to Peter Parker in *Spiderman*. Though Voltaire said it first and Luke (the apostle, not the Jedi) wrote, "From the one who has been entrusted with much, much more will be asked." But both of those sentiments sum up a lot of what Sun Tzu says in his book, and I'm going to do my best to echo that in mine.

Two obvious points worth mentioning before I go on: First, your students are not going to be done "learning to write" at the end of your course. A good composition class is simply the start. You can't turn water into wine in one semester, but be aware that your students will be moving in one direction or another after completing your class. They will either appreciate writing more or less, think more or less clearly and critically, and be more or less willing to deal with complexity. Your job is to get them moving in the right direction, to know enough and care enough to keep going. To what end? Well, there's probably never an end to one's growth as a writer. As long as one keeps writing.

The second thing to keep in mind is that the over-whelming majority of your students won't follow in your footsteps, won't become writers, scholars, critics, or (holy of holies) composition instructors. This doesn't diminish the importance of writing in their lives. Everyone has a different path to follow, challenges to overcome, and ways to impact the world. Your job is to give your students the skills to navigate those paths and overcome those challenges in the best ways possible.

One more thing before I proceed: Sun Tzu discusses ways to maximize the efforts and efficiency of his own troops and advice on how to defeat the enemy. I go back and forth between these two types of advice because it's all useful for us as composition teachers. We have our own troops (our students) and a powerful enemy (Bad Writing). And sometimes our students act like enemies or they come into the semester thinking they are our enemies. But they are not really enemies, to be defeated, they are really soldiers in training, people you need to bring over to your side. Always think of all your students as soldiers or potential soldiers, because if you perform as a leader should, eventually, they will be on your squad. Sometimes (rarely) you will have students who seem determined to really be enemies, who want to remain in an adversarial state, and I will discuss how to deal with them later in the book.

So, as I said, as a composition teacher, you need to view yourself as a leader. Even if you haven't gone through life thinking of yourself as a leader, if you've been content to sit back and observe, keep your thoughts to yourself, and dole out your charisma only when necessary, you're a leader now, in your classes at least. It doesn't matter what you do with the rest of your time, how you act as a student, friend, rugby player, or macramé whiz. In class, *you* are in charge.

So what traits do you need to succeed? Sun Tzu says that in order to lead troops effectively, a general needs to exhibit wisdom, credibility, benevolence, courage, and discipline. These make sense on a battlefield, but what do they mean when teaching a composition class?

1. Wisdom: you must know what good writing is and how one goes about producing it,
2. Credibility: your students must trust that you know what you're doing, know how to write, how to teach, and how to help others succeed,
3. Benevolence: your students should have no doubt that you genuinely want to help them learn and grow,
4. Courage: you must have faith in The Way; you must *believe* that good writing is important and be willing to stand up for it, even when met with opposing forces,
5. Discipline: you must establish rules and enforce them, with consequences for those who don't follow the rules.

Sun Tzu also says an effective leader "does not advance to seek glory (and) does not withdraw to avoid punishment, but cares for only the people's security and promotes the people's interests." He says a leader like this is "the nation's treasure." Have you ever thought of yourself as

your "nation's treasure?" Even as your school's or department's treasure? Well, you can be a treasure in all these
ways if you teach composition the way Sun Tzu would
have. This means you care first and foremost about what
your students do and learn. If helping your students is not
your main goal, you won't do your best and this job will
probably wear you down. If you want to be a "treasure,"
you need to realize how lucky you are to have been given
the opportunity to teach composition. In order for this to
work, you have to *want* to teach it.

Need a little more motivation? Okay, I'm going to
assume that you've lived enough life to know you have a
responsibility to your fellow human beings, that this is part
of being human. I'm also going to guess you've been met
with circumstances in life when you wanted to help someone, but couldn't, because you didn't have the knowledge,
resources, or whatever was needed at the time. When you
are teaching, it's all different. You have a class full of people
who *need* your help. You've got the knowledge, the tools,
and the authority to help them. What an opportunity!
You'd be a fool not to make the most of it. And if you're
not ready to make that jump, you can at least acknowledge
that to *not* do what you can to help your students, your
fellow human beings who need your help, would be just
plain selfishness. And you are not a selfish person, are you?
I didn't think so.

Sun Tzu says a good general's soldiers "may be given
death, or . . . given life, but there is no fear of danger and
betrayal." This means that no matter the circumstances,
your students should never fear you. They should respect

you, and in many ways submit to your wishes, do what you ask them to do, but this needs to be based on them trusting you and knowing you have their best interests at heart. Your attitude towards the teaching of the class and your students is important because it has a direct effect not only on how your students see you, but how they will perform.

If they don't see you as a compassionate, benevolent leader working for their success, they may think all the work you have them do for class is just to keep them busy, control them, or show them how ignorant they are. Some will assume low grades are motivated by your personal bias. They might take your feedback on their work as evidence you simply don't "like" them, are out to beat them. But if they know you are looking out for their best interests, they'll see that everything is for their benefit and they'll accept criticism, admit ignorance, and be more willing to do the work you need them to do to succeed and grow.

Now some of you may be thinking, this sounds like it's going to be way too much work. I don't mind teaching, but I've got my own life to live, my own goals to accomplish. Rest assured, I know we all need balance in our lives. But teaching will take time, whether you do it properly or not. If you follow Sun Tzu's principles, you will end up doing less work, not more. And every class you teach, every student, will provide you another opportunity to learn and grow and ultimately succeed, not only in the teaching of the class, but at whatever else you want to succeed at. Teaching well not only benefits your students, it benefits you too.

If you've still got reservations, I understand. But keep reading and you'll see how to be a more effective teacher without knocking yourself out, by doing *less* work. Sun Tzu explains the strategies of an effective leader in detail, and I will too, but before we get into those, I want to reiterate how you should view yourself: as a wise, credible, benevolent, courageous, disciplined general in the army of The Way.

Let me say that one more time: you are a wise, credible, benevolent, courageous, disciplined general in the army of The Way. This is the root from which everything else must grow.

How To Present Yourself

One of the most famous lines in *The Art of War* is "Warfare is the Way of deception." This is true for you too, especially when it comes to presenting yourself. But don't worry, this deception isn't at odds with your moral purpose. Because when Sun Tzu talks about deception, he is not saying one should be dishonest, lie, or hurt anyone. His advice is to be a "formless" leader as a means of always keeping the upper hand, with the balance of power in your control. What does it mean to be formless, or use deception?

Deception for your purposes means sometimes you've got to lead by standing back, teaching your students by putting them in positions to figure things out on their own and do the work they need to do to grow as writers. From the start, your students will be trying to "figure you out," which means watching for signs of strength and weakness, measuring your abilities, trying to discover your strategies (and then planning their own countermoves and shortcuts). While you must be transparent about some things—course goals, assignment requirements, due dates, attendance and grading policies, this is not a matter of revealing *yourself.* All semester long, there are going to be two of you: one in your head (observing your students, making plans, adapting to change, devising new strategies) and one the students see (standing in front of class, handing out assignment sheets, asking questions, leading discussions, engaging in a little friendly banter, providing comments and grades on their papers). While these are both you, they are not the same you, and your success as a teacher will depend a great deal on your ability to surprise your students, implement unorthodox strategies, and get them to figure things out on their own and do things they didn't realize they could do. It might seem easier to simply *tell* them what to do, but they won't learn that way.

But before I get too far explaining this deception as a means of getting your students to engage with the work of the class, I want to make clear there are some qualities students appreciate in their teachers and these are things you *don't* want to hide. Make it clear to them you have these qualities.

First of all, your students need you to be a good communicator. All your wisdom and compassion does them no good if they are not aware of it. I know a lot of great writers and thinkers who are not great speakers. Maybe you are one of them. And while you don't have to be great, you must, at the very least, speak clearly and loudly enough in class—a mumbling genius is no better than a hmmbllgeness. You also need to be clear about what you are saying. Ideas and information may seem obvious to you, but oversimplify it for your students. Get in the habit of writing down the most important things you want to convey in a class session and refer back to those notes throughout the class. Repeat information. Don't underestimate your students' ability to misunderstand you.

Secondly, students like energy and enthusiasm. This doesn't mean you are jumping around and performing tricks for them (though I'm sure they'd appreciate that). It means you're genuinely invested in the class, the material, and their success. Of course, never say or make it seem you are working *just* for their benefit. People don't want to be led by a martyr, see anyone suffering for them. When you are in class, they want to believe that there is no place you would rather be, nothing you would rather be talking about than writing.

How do you show this to them? One easy way to do this is by looking at writing samples you like—then talking about what you like about them and explaining why—letting them see your mind at work. This is simply modeling the behavior you want them to engage in. Early in the semester, I like to hand out and then have us read aloud (having students read one paragraph at a time, which I have found is a good use of class time as it again gets students used to speaking in class while reading closely and hearing what good writing sounds like) a short essay, like Bertrand Russell's "The Happy Life." I love this little essay about the path to happiness being the one that looks outward, borne from the desire to help others, because I believe it's true, and the six hundred or so words are so concise and precise, with lines like, "What a person needs for happiness is not self-denial, but that kind of direction of interest outward which will lead spontaneously and naturally to the same acts that a person absorbed in the pursuit of his own virtue could perform only by means of conscious self-denial." I can explain some words to my students, words they should know, like "hedonist" and "antithesis." And I like to discuss the figurative language he uses so well when he says that a person who has found this way to happiness "comes to feel him or herself part of the stream of life, not a hard separate entity like a billiard ball, which can have no relation with other such entities except that of collision." "Stream of life" may be familiar, I'll say, but describing billiard balls colliding with each other to capture how people interact, that's great! When I read that, I can feel the smooth veneer of the balls, hear the crack of the collisions between them that I've heard in so many bars and basements over my life. I'll explain to them that Russell says some people are like that too, never letting anyone in, never giving any part of themselves to others, and as a result, these people are not happy.

In the twenty minutes it takes to read over something like this and then discuss style, tone, metaphors, theme, and the like, I can show them not only how to read, but how to get caught up in it. And the more my students see it matters to me, the better chance I've got of making it matter to them.

I often do a reading and discussion like this later in the semester too, when I think the class needs a little change of pace, something unexpected, or when I have recently read something in a magazine or journal that is relevant for us and something they'll be able to relate to (this obviously changes depending on the other course readings we have done).

Another thing you can do to share your enthusiasm about writing (and develop theirs) is ask them to show you pieces of writing they like. One day early in the semester, ask them all to bring in a short work they like. Then give them some time to write about *why* they like it, and to speculate on how it was put together. Then have some of them explain this to their classmates.

I've found this strategy to be more interesting and useful than starting by providing instructions on "how to write" and defining the various pieces and parts of an essay. I mean, great cooks don't become great cooks by simply following recipes—first, they fall in love with food, then they figure out how the food was prepared, then they try to create their own. Writing works the same way.

You can also give them the choice to bring in something they *don't* like and explain their reasons why—this can be just as valuable. In both cases, it is important to have genuine conversations about what they have shared with the class, to develop everyone's understanding of good and bad and different types of writing. This also reinforces the idea that you are interested in their thoughts on writing.

Students also appreciate a sense of fairness; they need to know you have a sympathetic attitude towards them and won't play favorites. Of course, you can't come into a classroom the first day and say to a bunch of strangers, "I want you all to succeed because I care about all of you!" While it may be true in some ways, it'll come off as disingenuous and they won't trust you. And you can't just *tell* them you care, you need to *show* it. But don't try to show this on the first day, or in the first week. In fact, my advice is to not try at all. Let it come clear naturally as the class proceeds. Early in the semester, you can establish the fact that you are sympathetic *to their situation* (their situation of being busy students and developing writers) just by talking about these things in class. Letting them know that you understand they exist outside of class, and have got other classes, other interests, jobs, families, are on sports teams, are commuters, live in the dorms, et cetera, goes a long way in winning them over. Perhaps later in the semester, when you're having an individual conference with a student you've gotten to know over the course of the semester, then you can honestly say, "I want *you* to succeed. I care about *you* achieving your goals." But by the time you say this, your students should already know it. And they should also know that you could say the exact same thing to all of your students and mean it.

As far as the writing goes, always let them know you know where they are coming from, that you understand writing is hard work. Never say to them, "Just do it." Never say, "It's easy." Let them know that even the most successful writers have to work at it. Tell them writing guru William Zinsser said, "If writing seems hard, it's because it is hard. It's one of the hardest things people do." Or tell them that Thomas Mann said, "A writer is a person for whom writing is more difficult than it is for other people." I also like Hemingway's "We are all apprentices in a craft where no one reaches mastery." Hearing this from successful writers (and you might have to explain who Zinsser, Mann, and Hemingway *are*) helps them see that their struggles are universal, which can be a great relief to them as well as a confidence builder.

Of course, it's not enough to just expose them to these nuggets of wisdom. I like to have them do something with them, for example, passing out a sheet with eight or ten of these writing quotes, break the class into small groups, assign each group one of the quotes and five minutes to run it through their minds and find a way to explain it.

Here's a handout (with more of my favorite quotes) that I'll share with the class on the day we do an exercise like this:

- -

Writing Quotes for Group Discussion/Analysis

How can I know what I think till I see what I say?
(E.M. Forster)

The act of putting pen to paper encourages pause for thought, this in turn makes us think more deeply about life, which helps us regain our equilibrium.
(Norbet Platt)

Work on a good piece of writing proceeds on three levels: a musical one, where it is composed; an architectural one, where it is constructed; and finally, a textile one, where it is woven.
(Walter Benjamin)

Anyone who says writing is easy isn't doing it right.
(Amy Joy)

If writing didn't require thinking then we'd all be doing it.
(Jeremiah Laabs)

If a man means his writing seriously, he must mean to write well. But how can he write well until he learns to see what he has written badly. His progress toward good writing and his recognition of bad writing are bound to unfold at something like the same rate.
(John Ciardi)

I write entirely to find out what I'm thinking, what I'm looking at, what I see and what it means.
(Joan Didion)

The only time I know that something is true is the moment I discover it in the act of writing.
(Jean Malaquais)

- -

After each group has discussed their quote, we will reconvene as a class, then one member of the group will typically read the quote and I'll ask the others to explain the group's understanding of what it means. I have found a good prompt is asking them to "Give us the highlights of your group's discussion."

These quotes can also be used effectively as reflective writing prompts, asking students to discuss their writing experiences in the context of one of the quotes. Other times I have my students read short essays on writing by

Annie Dillard or William Stafford or Peter Elbow, which serve the same dual purpose—give them some insight on writing and the process as well as an opportunity to engage in analysis.

Because writing is not easy, your students will make mistakes, but it is important to show them that it is part of the process, essential to their growth. If you really want them to become writers, you need to get them to embrace the idea that to mess up and flounder is often the path to success. They'll get frustrated along the way, but you need to make sure it's for the right reasons—because they are having a hard time finding the right words, putting them in the right order, knowing which ones to leave in and take out. If they get frustrated with that, that's good. They'll work through it. They'll learn. But if they get frustrated with you, for the wrong reasons, you risk losing them, and once you lose students, there's no getting them back. They may tolerate you, they may do the work, but you need them to do more than that to achieve the goals you're aiming them towards.

One thing that will make your job easier is the fact that many of your students will have had some history of strict teachers—which means most will generally behave and listen to you even if you are not "strict." Of course, I don't mean to say that your class should be too loose. It should be comfortable, but run efficiently. Your students should show respect by listening to what you say and doing what you ask them to do. And of course, the class won't be easy—you'll craft assignments that are challenging and don't allow easy ways out. You must ask a lot of them and promote high expectations because people generally don't find success by accident—it takes effort, and there needs to be a reason to succeed. Just about all examples of human ingenuity have been borne out of necessity. The people who invented the wheel, indoor plumbing, weapons, medicine, even the notion that a bouquet of flowers can serve as a romantic gesture, did so because they felt they *had* to, not just because they had some time on their hands. So you need to be demanding—demanding that they think and write and work and revise. You need to demand hard work. But this doesn't mean you have to be too hard-nosed with them. Other teachers may be, and your students have surely been beaten down already—but you can show them the light: *Hey, school and life and thinking and hard work can be interesting and satisfying!* Always remember the goal: to get your students to gain a new vision—to see writing, the world, and themselves in different ways.

Students also need to know that you know what you're talking about. This doesn't mean you need to tell them about your dissertation (please, don't), but as you move through class, your knowledge and preparedness should be evident. You don't ever want to give your students the impression you don't know what you're doing. Everyone's life is made up of time, and nobody wants to waste it, not eighteen-year-old students who think the easy way is the best way, not older, nontraditional students coming to class after long days of work. You need to make every minute count—in the classroom and in the work they do outside of class. Everything needs to be purposeful because what even lazy people find more distasteful than hard work is busy work, in your case assignments or exercises with no clear purpose, the kind that just seem to be killing time.

I'd say most students will come into the semester *wanting* to trust you, *expecting* you to know your stuff. This is good. Don't give them any opportunity to think otherwise. If you ever find yourself feeling like you're foundering (let's face it, we're not perfect and will run into trouble), don't get nervous. Whether they ask questions about grammar rules, MLA format, university policies, or the existence of life on other planets, provide the best answer you can, and if it's really not important, redirect their attention. If it is, suspend discussion and say you need more time to investigate the question further. Encourage them to do the same. And be sure to follow through on this. Not having all the answers is not necessarily a bad thing. It gives you another opportunity to model the kind of behavior you want your students to emulate.

I am also going to say that you should not try to look too smart in front of your students. Don't try to impress them. If you are the smartest person in the room (and in most cases, you will be), it will become evident with no effort on your part. Conversely, if you *try* to look smart, especially at the beginning of the semester, it will only build resistance, the wrong kind of barrier between you and them. Now, you might, as some teachers have before you, walk into the classroom thinking: "What a lucky bunch of students, to have *me* as their teacher." You might think to yourself as they embark on some rudimentary exercise: "Do these kids know how brilliant I am, the kinds of writing and thinking *I'm* capable of?" The answer, of course, is no, they don't, and more importantly, for this class, for these purposes, it doesn't matter.

Whatever your intentions in becoming a teacher were, I'm sure one was not to lord your brilliance over a bunch of composition students, whether they are nontraditional students with kids at home and bills to pay, or homesick college adolescents with anxiety and acne who are pining for boyfriends or girlfriends back home or are simply feeling lonely or displaced, struggling to adjust to cafeteria food. If you've got credentials and ambitions, that's great. You can mention this if you can't help yourself. But it really doesn't matter in the composition classroom. To focus attention on that would be to focus attention on yourself—the absolute wrong place.

Ideally, your students won't even realize you're teaching them. Sun Tzu says, "Perceiving a victory when it is perceived by all is not the highest victory." This means you need to forget about your ego and getting credit from everyone. If your students get to the end of the semester and think to themselves, "My writing has really improved and I did it all myself," then you've succeeded. The best teachers give their students the impression not only that they (the students) have figured things out on their own, but (in some ways at least) they ultimately know more than their teacher. Let them believe this. Don't let your ego get in the way of doing your job.

So I am telling you to be enthusiastic, fair, and competent. I'm saying don't try to look smart or be a hard-ass. It's also important that you are not a phony. Whenever possible, speak in class as if you are having a conversation, not enacting a performance. Students can sniff out inauthenticity and hate hypocrites. Be honest. Be forthright.

Besides improving as writers, as in having developed the ability to write a better paper, essay, email, or whatever, my goal is that my students leave the class with a better attitude towards writing and a desire to continue to improve. I like to think that all my students, even those whose experience in composition class was not revelatory, will some years after the fact, when they've grown in knowledge and wisdom, have continued to develop as writers and thinkers, and look back and say, "Oh, that was a very beneficial class." I don't know if this ever happens, and maybe it's just a fantasy I've devised to help me deal with some of the angst of the job, but I always tell myself at the end of the semester, amidst the flurry of deadlines and workloads, that most of my students won't realize how they've changed, how the class has helped, and that's okay with me. As long as I know they have changed.

But, you may be asking, how can I be honest and deceptive (formless) at the same time? Well, Sun Tzu says you should be like water, because "water's formation adapts to the enemy to achieve victory." This may be a matter of adapting your assignment sequence if you feel students aren't ready to move on. If they are frustrated with something related to the class—grades, the workload, failure to see the point of it all—you can talk about that. Even better, have them write about it. If something is happening in society (a pandemic or protests for equality, for example), or on campus (the president is stepping down, a big party got busted), and they are all talking about that and want to think about that instead of what you have planned, have them talk about it and write about it. Try to relate that topic to one you have already discussed. This is using the energy they bring to class for your purposes, adapting to their formation.

Another way to "adapt to the enemy" is to have your students view something you see as essential through a lens they are familiar with. For example, when I wanted my students to get a better understanding of Nietzsche's argument in "Morality as Anti-Nature," an essay about how religious rules of morality are at odds with one's natural instincts, and ultimately harmful to humanity, after they had read it, instead of jumping right into a discussion, I had them work in groups to create a social media profile for him, with likes and dislikes, relationship status, things he likes, et cetera. They thought it was fun, they were working on familiar territory, but to do this well and explain why they created the profile they had, they not only had to read Nietzsche closely but think critically and creatively too.

Though it may sound contradictory, formlessness is how you can gain control of the classroom. Sun Tzu explains this when he says, "If we can make the enemy show his position while we are formless, we will be at full force while the enemy is divided." The most important way to think of your students' formation is to think about their writing—attitudes, habits, and practices. You must discover what these are and act accordingly, steering them away from the bad and towards the good. Your goal for all your students is to help them become more effective, efficient writers, to get them to work, think, and write like they haven't before. You need to use your formlessness to trick them into working, especially early in the semester. By the end of the semester, I'm always delighted to find many students are taking the initiative and doing the work, going above and beyond: revising, researching, developing ideas, et cetera. This doesn't happen for all students, but it happens for enough to let me know I'm doing my job. And when students get to this point, working like writers, I don't have to worry about deception or formlessness—by that point, they are on my side, fighting for The Way.

Sun Tzu also says, "The place of battle must not be made known to the enemy." Keeping the place of battle unknown prevents them from building a solid defense. Adapted to the classroom, this means if they don't know what you're trying to do, they won't be able to defend against you. So while you should always know what you are doing, and *why*, your students shouldn't. While I give my students tasks with clear objectives, I do not always explain why they are doing them or how they fit into the goals of the class, as I think this can sometimes make it less interesting for them and thereby sap their energy.

For example, I don't think they'll be very interested if I tell them the objective is to "distinguish among ideas, concepts, theories, or practical approaches to a problem or question." But they will get interested if I show them two arguments on either side of an issue, whether it's animal research, social media use, virtual learning, or a liberal arts education, and ask them to make sense of the debate, or take a side, then the other. The assignments I give them, the specific tasks, need to be focused and interesting enough for them not to stop and ask, "What is the point of this?" How will you know if they are interesting? Well, I always ask myself if I would get bored completing the assignment. Would I have to think critically and creatively to complete it? If the answer is no, I come up with something better.

Sometimes, I will have a short review after students complete an assignment to explain to them what they just did and why it is important. For example, after my students create the profile for Nietzsche, I'll explain to them that they have "contextualized his work" and "identified biases." After I have them write a scene of dialogue between Machiavelli and Martin Luther King Jr., I'll explain that they were putting the arguments of two writers "in conversation" with each other. Whatever class you are teaching, there will be clearly defined objectives for the students. You can't ignore these. And I'm not telling you what these objectives should be or how to change them. I'm giving suggestions on how to achieve these goals in ways that will engage your students in ways that make the class more interesting for them and easier for you.

Sun Tzu explains how this works because "if he prepares to defend many places, then the forces will be few in number." Early in the semester, you should be bombarding your students with the questions and exercises in which they are forced to reveal themselves as writers and individuals, show their likes and dislikes, strengths and weaknesses, histories and goals, passions and fears. If you are genuinely curious about them, it's easy to come up with the right kinds of questions: "If you could be an animal, what would you be and why?" Or better than that: "Describe an unpleasant experience. If you had the ability to erase this from your memory, would you? Why or why not? How do you think your self would change if the memory was gone?" If they complete those, they've got no way around revealing themselves, and you'll figure them out, which increases your advantage. They'll think you're just giving them some provocative, enjoyable, but not very serious work. But while it may not all be "serious," all their writing should be intellectually stimulating, and all the while, you should be compiling valuable information, feeling them out, to help you develop your strategies for the rest of the semester.

Before I go on, I need to discuss the risk of being too formless. While it is counterproductive to wield too much control, it's also counterproductive to do the opposite. The best way to move through the semester is by creating the class *with* the students—getting their input, allowing some freedom in topics, coming to compromises, empowering them, teaching them to think for themselves and take responsibility for their work. While Sun Tzu's "formlessness" is something to strive for, some teachers, it seems, take this too far and end up being not just formless, but too passive, almost absent. Instead of being facilitators of learning, they position themselves as spectators in the class, watching to see what happens, providing little guidance or input. Until, of course, it comes time to grade papers, when the teacher's authority rules supreme. This is a philosophy some composition theorists believe in.

But I think it can lead to all kinds of trouble. Not only will students not learn, they'll get angry.

Instead of just telling you more about this, let me show you with some choice excerpts from emails sent to me (when I was Department Chair) by frustrated students in composition classes:

My English professor is failing to do his job as an instructor. Class has become something close to pointless to attend. We go to class and he usually is the last one in the classroom for starters. Then he asks, "What are we going to talk about? What did we talk about last time?" and the class remains silent until someone speaks up. The entire class is basically run off of how we want it ran. We have not really ever talked about anything about writing. We have not been taught in how to improve our writing. We go to class, he assigns a paper based on an essay, and we write about it. When we write a paper, he gives very little feedback and no grades. He has only graded two papers, and gave bad grades on them for reasons we do not know. He is vague on his responses. He has just been very irritable when it comes to our education, we are paying for this class and we are failing to learn anything from it.

Here's an email I received from the parent of a student in the same class:

I believe that freshman writing is one of the most important subjects for a student. My freshman writing class, when I was an undergraduate student, was excellent. As an attorney, I still use skills I learned in that class so long ago. We have been happy with all Michael's classes except this one. . . . The expectations for the writing class seem to be ambiguous. He did not receive any significant feedback on his writings until after the midterm grade was given. While the grade is important, even more important is that Michael learns something from the class. So far, that has been minimal. Michael can meet expectations when he knows what those expectations are and he is given feedback on what needs to be improved.

And finally, one more from another student from that class:

Since the beginning of the semester four essays have been assigned, all on the topic of education. I have no problem writing essays, in fact, I enjoy writing and get a lot of satisfaction out of writing a well written paper. The problem that I am having with this class is that, when he assigns an essay, there is no clear prompt that is given. When we question and ask what the prompt is, he tells us to read the background information that he gives us, and for the most part tells us to create our own prompt. In order to write our papers, our class collaborates on the side to figure out what to write about. When we write our essay rough drafts and turn them in, he says that we will receive a 100% as long as we have more than three sentences written on the page, or we will receive a zero if we don't turn it in at all. To me, it seems a rough draft is something that we should be receiving feedback on in order to make corrections and turn in a good paper when the final draft is due. Our professor gives us very little, if any feedback on our rough drafts and makes no comments about what to do better.... This frustrates me because I feel that an English professor is supposed to be here to help us and make us stronger writers, and he is not willing to help at all.... All in all, I feel like I am not learning anything in my English class and this frustrates me very much. I am paying to take this class and get an education and I feel as if my English professor is not doing his job at all.... I came to this college because I want to succeed. I am a hard worker and I take my education very seriously and feel as though my English Professor is certainly not on the same page with his students and does not care about the success of his students.

Okay, maybe this a worst-case scenario. But this serves as a great example of how *not* to teach the class. This guy had been teaching as long as I had (we'd been in graduate school together). And his failures were not simply the result of incompetence or laziness, because in the conversations I had with him about these concerns and his teaching philosophy in general, it was clear that this laissez-faire way of (not) doing things was the way he'd been taught to teach composition. He thought it would work. As I've already stated, I believe input from students is essential for a good writing class, but when taken to this extreme, the result seems to be little productivity and a lot of frustration. I mean, the very word "input" implies "putting in" to something, not completely creating on one's own, which is essentially what these students were asked to do. For a composition class, the teacher must provide the framework: clear objectives, assignment sheets, exercises, sample papers, et cetera. Just like preschool kids learn to build structures when they are given blocks, not when they are given nothing, our students must be given some things to work with. The students need to be taught.

As I'm sure you are wondering what happened with this class, after I sat and observed his class and we had some discussions about student complaints, he agreed his methods were not working and he'd change them. I followed up with some students later in the semester, and they said things had improved, though I doubt any of them had the most productive semesters they could have (maybe he just gave them all good grades so they would stop complaining). And I'm not sure how this instructor taught his classes after this one as he didn't teach for the department again. But I really hope, for his sake, and more so for the sake of his students, that he has changed, that he is doing more *teaching*.

So while you should regularly put students in positions to think for themselves, don't forget they also need guidance and direction. Sun Tzu says, "If an army is without its equipment (and) provisions (and) stores, it will lose." Soldiers need materials to do their jobs, and so do writers. This means you can't expect your students to do things you haven't yet taught them. If you haven't given them clear objectives, explained how a piece of writing is constructed and what it needs to say and do, many will founder (and be frustrated at your seeming incompetence or seethe at

what they perceive as your condescending inscrutabil-
ity). If they fail to properly include a quotation, or add an
example, or develop an idea, or anything you need them
to do to meet the goals of the class, if you haven't shown
them how to do it, it's your fault if they don't.

And remember it may take a few times to properly
"show" them something before they understand it. And it
may take a few attempts before they are able to do this
themselves. But make sure you are modeling the kind of
thinking and writing they need to do. Make sure you are
clearly communicating to them what they need to accomplish. You don't want to do the work for them, or be too
prescriptive. And sometimes the best ways to get them
to learn will be through asking questions and facilitating
discussions, not saying much at all, but when you look at
the big picture, remember that you know a lot more about
writing than they do and sometimes you've got to explain
things to them, especially when it comes to what they are
doing right and what they are doing wrong.

Sun Tzu also says, "To take advantage of the enemy's
lack of preparation, take unexpected routes to attack where
the enemy is not prepared." What do unexpected routes
look like in composition class? Well, asking surprising
questions (but not nonsensical ones) is good. For example,
if a class falls on Valentine's Day, if I'm not holding another
round of the Bad Love Poem contest (composed in small
groups and then read aloud in class), I have had students
answer one of these questions: "Does true love exist? Is it
better to have loved and lost or never loved at all? Why
do you think people in arranged marriages have higher

rates of marriage satisfaction and lower rates of divorce?"
Leading them to connect their writing to life outside class
and school is important.

Your students' lack of preparation is something you
have got to take advantage of to be successful. And in this
case, by lack of preparation I don't mean not doing the
reading or the work assigned. They have got to do that.
I'm thinking about what you'll ask them to do with the
reading or do with the assignment. The first time you can
take advantage is on day one. Think about it, when you
step into the classroom, you'll have spent time and energy
preparing for the class, the semester, and your students will
just show up. If they're prepared in any way, it's to brace
themselves against another one of the same old classes
they've had in the past. By showing them that this will not
be the case, you are immediately in a position of control,
and once you've got it, you've got to take advantage of it.

For example, I recently had my students read Sherry
Turkle's "Stop Googling. Let's Talk," an article on cell phone
and social media addiction and how it is affecting communication and relationships. This was something nearly all of
them, avid smartphone users, could relate to. And though
some resisted the article's main points about the resulting
inability to effectively mull things over in one's mind (that
is, have conversations with one's self) and have meaningful conversations with others, one student admitted aloud,
six or seven weeks into her freshman year, that because
of her and her peers' reliance on smartphones and social
media, she hadn't had a "real" conversation with anyone
on campus since the semester began. This was not only a

powerful statement that really highlighted the seriousness of the issue, the fact that she was willing to admit this in class made it clear she trusted me and her classmates and felt safe expressing herself.

It's important to allow them to have freedom and make connections, but you still need to direct *how* they write about things. You just can't let them freewrite, ramble, or spit out some of the same old stuff they've written before. The goal is to make all their writing an act of discovery in one way or another—discovery about the topic, themselves, or writing. Questions like "Why do people like to go to zoos?" Or "Why do people like to have pets?" leads them to the kind of change you want for them because it leads them to think about familiar topics and their own experiences in new ways, leads them to make connections they may not have considered before. *Why* questions are usually the best for getting students to think, to have to consider multiple perspectives, especially when there are lots of possible answers. I have had students take questions like these and turn them into full research papers. One student wrote a very interesting paper not only explaining some of the reasons why people have pets, but arguing that for some it served as a social crutch, cutting them off from genuine human interaction.

Sun Tzu says another way to achieve formlessness is "If able, appear unable." This doesn't mean you want to appear ignorant; as discussed earlier, you need to establish credibility so your troops will have faith in you. But you do not want to establish yourself as the authority for all things in class because this will stifle your students' ability to grow. You do not want to simply *tell* your students how to write—you need to put them in positions to figure it out themselves. There are countless ways to write well—one would be truly ignorant to think otherwise, or assume knowledge of them all. Still, how does one appear "unable" while still teaching the class? Well, when you're reading a sample essay, for example, don't tell your students that the introduction is strong, or that the thesis statement is underdeveloped, or the organization is faulty. Simply ask them these questions—as if you have no idea what the answers are. If a good rule of writing is "Show, don't Tell," a good rule of teaching writing may be "Ask, don't Tell." When you read sample drafts together, even if you have read them ahead of time and know what points you want to discuss, say, "I'm not sure what to make of this," then break them into groups, give them questions, let them work a while, then begin your discussion. Of course, with your experience, at a glance you'll be able to identify the strengths and weaknesses of a paper, the ways it meets or fails to meet the goals of the assignment, but your job is to draw your students into seeing the same things. And you will also be surprised to find that your students can see other things too, make their own discoveries in addition to your own.

Sun Tzu also says, "If active, appear not active." Behind the scenes, you'll be busy enough—planning, plotting, preparing; but in the classroom, everything should appear to happen as naturally as water dripping off a leaf. You should move from one lesson to the next, then the next, and so on until class time is over. But it should seem to your students that this was not your "plan" exactly, rather that it all transpired organically, and have them thinking things like: "Once we figured out that the thesis statement was underdeveloped, we could see why the essay got off track and why that example on page two didn't work, and then that exercise on opening paragraphs was helpful, and so was the one on 'Showing, not Telling,' and this is all starting to make sense to me now." Of course, these were the points you planned to make, but instead of writing them on the board and saying, "This is what we are going to cover today," maybe all you did was ask them, "How well do you think this example of the monkey with the cell phone works with the rest of the essay?" This brings up another thing: When the class is doing analysis or critiques, it's important to not always start at the beginning, because that's too predictable.

Of course, you can't start in the way I just described and have all those productive conversations if you haven't already clearly conveyed to them the purpose of the introduction, the thesis statement, body paragraphs, supporting evidence, specific examples, et cetera. But after they've gotten that, after you have established a common vocabulary and understanding of what good writing is, you can start them anywhere and they'll see how all the parts of a piece of writing work together or how they don't. And the latter is more likely early in the semester and in some ways more valuable than a "model" paper because, as you surely know, we learn best from mistakes.

Another piece of Sun Tzu's advice on formlessness is "If near, appear far." As I said earlier, the teacher they see is not the teacher you are. For example, if you're having a class discussion and you can sense a student is about to make an important point (as in, "This introduction is interesting, but doesn't really fit with the topic of the paper"), don't say so. Instead, keep asking questions. Wait and see where the student is going. Make him or her explain it to you. "What do you mean? *Why* doesn't it work?" You'll be surprised how often they can say it better than you could have. And having students answer questions and say the right things is often a lot more valuable than if you had said them yourself. Students often trust each other more than they trust you, and good students can serve as models and inspiration for others, motivating them in ways you can't. As much as your students may come to appreciate you, you are always on the other side of the desk, not one of them.

Sometimes you'll ask questions and the student who answers will be objectively wrong. What to do then? It's good to nod your head, not in agreement with what the student said, of course, but to acknowledge you've understood the point the student was trying to make, validate it (every voice matters!), but then respond with another question, or maybe rephrase the question you started with. At the same time, look around the room for someone to jump in. Sometimes you'll get a volunteer. Other times you'll see a light in a student's eyes that indicates knowledge of the answer you are looking for. Other times you might have to call on a student you know will get it right, coax it out of another, or, as a last resort only, state the truth yourself. For example, I like to assign my students to read and write about Emerson's "Self-Reliance." I'm going to refer to this essay a lot, not because I think everyone should assign it, or because it's an essential reading for your class, but more to simplify my explanations so I don't have to summarize a bunch of different essays for you. However, I do like using it for my composition classes because it is somewhat challenging (written in 1841) and because Emerson's argument about trusting and relying on one's self and resisting the conformist influences of society strikes a chord with many of them and they are able to relate it to their own lives and the world around them. But some students are critical of Emerson's argument because they believe he is proposing selfishness and anarchy, and they believe that someone like Hitler is a perfect example of Emerson's self-reliant person because he just did what he felt was right, with horrendous consequences, and therefore, they conclude Emerson is all wrong.

But this is ignoring key parts of Emerson's idealistic view of humanity, which assumes all people are pure and good and generous in their heart of hearts and it's evil influences (most notably, for Emerson, society) that degrade people and make them destructive. So while Hitler is not conforming to others, he is not self-reliant in the way Emerson explains it.

This question (and answer) is valuable in our discussion of "Self-Reliance," and so I try to incorporate it in one form or another every semester. I know the answer but appear "far" by asking the students, "Was Hitler self-reliant?" By pretending I don't know the answer, I force them to think about it. And even if I do have to state the answer at the end of this long process, after much discussion, it will stick with them much better than if I'd just come out and stated it early on, because the topic will have been rolling around their heads for five to ten minutes, creating tension, and once that tension is resolved, that satisfaction will help it to stick.

Your Students

Now that you know some ways to see yourself, how should you view your students, those disinterested-looking, glassy-eyed strangers? First, let me tell you how *not* to see them.

Do not view them as inferior. While it's true they may be younger or less experienced than you (in writing, education, and life) and perhaps misguided (about writing, education, and life), that's not their fault, is it? I've seen teachers get upset with their students for their ignorance—but how can they be upset about this? No one knows everything. And while it's true some people pick up things, like writing, more easily than others, their ignorance is the very reason they are in your class. The faults they have are the very ones they're asking you to help them overcome. Let me say that again: They are asking for your help. Now they might not use these words, may not seem enthralled with everything you say, and may not gush about how much they value your efforts. Some may skip class, complain about assignments, make excuses, and take every shortcut possible. But by registering for your class, whether it is required or not, they are acknowledging that they need help of some kind. This is the essential dynamic of the relationship. They want and need help, and you are there to provide it. So don't look down on them—it's smart to ask for help when one needs it.

It's also important you don't view your students as competitors. Teaching is not a zero-sum game. If a student fails, the teacher hasn't "won," in the same way a student getting an "A" hasn't "beaten" the teacher. Generally, if a student succeeds (in this case, writes papers that meet or exceed the goals of the course), both student and teacher have succeeded. Likewise, if a student fails, the teacher has also failed (yes, it's not always the teacher's fault, but it is still failure). The key point here is that viewing the semester as a fight between you and your students guarantees you will all lose, waste everyone's time and energy, stunt your students' growth, and teach them the wrong things.

The goal for the semester, of course, is for you *and* your students to win. If there is a loser, it is Bad Writing—sloppy thinking, generalizations, clichés, laziness, the first draft. Bad Writing is the true enemy, and sometimes it manifests itself in your students. But don't hold this against them. Don't see them and their inadequacies as one in the same. Don't think, as some teachers do, that students are *trying* to write poorly—as if they turn in their papers thinking, "Good luck making sense of this!" Now, while it's true some may not be doing all they can to write well, I'm almost certain that none put forth the effort to *try* to write poorly. Only a writter that knows what they're doing could "throw down' a sentence that drawers attention to for it's deficiencies weaknesses & etc. mistakes and your students ain't like that!

So your assumption, at least early in the semester, should be that they are doing the best they can. Don't attribute bad writing to a lack of effort until you know for sure that is the case (and if that is the case, there are ways to deal with that).

What a job, you may sometimes be thinking, what a life. All my education, my training, my experience, all my hours of hard work has banished me to hours of reading sloppy, underdeveloped, banal, or incomprehensible papers? Yes, it has, and you need to embrace it. While you should always ready yourself to be surprised and impressed by your students, it's important to accept the fact that you'll be collecting papers that need work from writers that need help. If you come to the realization that what you're really interested in is reading great stuff, beautifully written, with keen insights into big ideas, by all means, you should do it. Those works are out there. There are already more written than you will ever have time to read. But that's called *reading*, not teaching, and what your students need is a *teacher*.

It is also important you don't get angry with your students. Even if you utilize all of Sun Tzu's principles to your advantage and become a more efficient and effective teacher, you may still get tired, or frustrated, or feel unappreciated, but getting angry at your students will only make things worse. Can you be upset if your students don't try? Yes. If they don't listen, if they don't take your advice when they revise? Yes, but to a large extent, these faults will be your fault, too, because you haven't gotten them fully invested in their writing, haven't shown them the value of The Way. So if you're going to get angry at them, you will have to get angry with yourself too. And who wants to spend time being angry? Not you. You know how great you can be when you're in a good mood, the way you can light up a room. You won't be like that if you're angry. And if you think you can be angry with your students but turn it off with your colleagues, friends, family, and self, you can't. Anger doesn't work like that. It's either there or it's not. And if you get your students properly invested in the work, in the writing, they will try, they will listen, they will revise. But confrontation, competition, anger, resentment, superiority, condescension, spite—avoid these at all costs. See your students as who they truly are—volunteer soldiers who have signed up to fight for The Way.

Now I am not saying you need to "like" all your students personally, or even equally. There are always some students that are more like you than others, that have the same hobbies, interests, or worldviews. You can use this to your advantage, but your relationships with them shouldn't be too personal. You can be friendly, but the key dynamic needs to be student-teacher. I'm not saying shut off your emotions, but be aware of them. If you aren't, you risk losing your ability to teach effectively. And on the other hand, if you feel you *don't* like some of them, or you only like the strong writers, the ones who make your job "easier," you won't be as effective as you need to be. Resist this by viewing them all as equals, all as apprentice writers, and open your heart, as it were, to all of them. Give them all your best efforts.

Sun Tzu says, "If you know the enemy and know yourself, the victory is not at risk." So besides having these right attitudes towards your students, you also need to understand them. Keep in mind that each student will bring unique strengths and weaknesses to class. You need to take advantage of these strengths or put them in a position to overcome these weaknesses, but you can't do that unless you identify them first. That is, to teach your students effectively, you've got to spend some time getting to know them. Each and every one. As quickly as possible. That may seem a daunting task, but it's not that difficult. But before I explain how to do that, I'll share what I think are some general truths about composition students, characteristics many have in common:

1. Most will not willingly place themselves in the types of complex, sometimes thorny intellectual mazes that you need them to get caught up in, the kind you have probably grown comfortable in. By the end of the semester, you want them to be able to read a challenging essay and respond to it in a way that not only makes sense of it but goes beyond the obvious and adds something new to the conversation. Most first-year composition students won't have experience with this kind of challenge or know how to proceed. If you give them an assignment like this early on, they may not be totally confused, but they'll just look for a right or wrong answer, or try to figure out what it is they think you want them to say. They'll stay on the safest ground possible. Your goals are to get them to venture beyond that, to appreciate complexity, to discover and situate their thoughts in relation to others, to develop and

articulate arguments of some sort, to take chances with their writing, to say something new. But remember, it's the rare student who will walk into the classroom at the start of the semester ready to do this. For the others, the overwhelming majority, you need to teach them how to do this.

2. Not only will your students stay on safe ground, they will generally take the easiest path provided to them. They have been taught in algebra that the shortest distance between two points is a straight line, and, if you allow it, you will see lots of straight lines in composition class, doing superficial readings, giving superficial responses, cutting straight to the chase, failing to develop their thoughts. Many of them have been rewarded for basic, generic writing in previous classes. The key is to not allow this by posing the right kinds of questions, by giving them the right kinds of assignments. Don't assume your students will challenge themselves, especially early in the semester. Keep all this in mind when you craft your assignments. If you give them a simple question, they'll give you simple answers, won't grow as writers, and it will be your fault.

For example, instead of asking, "Gun control: for or against?" or "Gun control: how do you feel about it?" ask them, "Why are some people so opposed to gun control? Are their concerns valid? Why or why not?" Or maybe "If guns are not the problem behind the number of gun deaths in America, why do countries with fewer guns have fewer gun deaths per capita (and fewer overall murders in any form)?" Questions like these make sure the easiest path you allow is not an easy one. To answer the questions like these, they need to do the work you want them to do (though I'm sure you can get them writing about more interesting, original topics than gun control).

Also keep in mind that students of this age and experience (traditional college students, that is) are often easily distracted, have a lot on their minds, are taking other (often demanding) classes at the same time as yours. Sometimes they are assigned to write scores of papers for other classes, from teachers who don't understand writing instruction, with no class time dedicated to discussing writing. This means they're going to try to churn those out, relying on the bad habits and strategies they've started the semester with. These are all challenges you must overcome to do your job well.

3. In general, new college students are also resistant to authority. If you are teaching traditional students, you'll be meeting many of your students at the point in their lives where they see themselves as finally free from parental rules, school rules, social rules. They want to be independent, and not only that, they want you to know they are independent. If you are teaching older students, many will be set in their ways, have long histories of making decisions for themselves, and may not like the idea of someone seemingly very different than themselves telling them what to do. Either way, if you think, like some teachers do, that your number one goal is to let them know who's in charge, you can accomplish that by barking out orders and letting them know you don't want to hear excuses. But that's not going to work because they'll tune you out, do what they can to avoid punishment, but never really grow.

Of course, it's not that simple. No army succeeds if the general is not in charge, and so while you'll give them some freedom, grant them the illusion of independence in class, and work *with* them, you'll also always be in charge in the sense that they will be moving in the direction you need them to be. My main point here is to let you know that their resistance is natural. Don't be surprised by it. Later, I'll explain how some resistance can actually provide energy for the class—if used in the right ways.

4. Another thing to keep in mind is that many students will walk into your class nervous and anxious—about writing, college, life in general. They're usually first-year college students and have no idea what to expect. They haven't been, like many of you, in college classrooms for the better part of their adult lives. They may also not know another person in class, sometimes another person in the entire school. Goal Number One is getting them comfortable. The sooner you can convey a calm confidence and put them at ease (though obviously not to the point they are so relaxed they are not paying attention), the sooner you can begin to teach them about writing. And it's not that hard if you know your stuff, are prepared, and genuinely want to help.

To sum up this section rather bluntly, your students may be simple, lazy, resistant to authority, and anxious. But know that once you show them you've got their best interests at heart, they'll get comfortable and you can start to teach them. How do you do this? Well, besides natural expressions of your general magnanimity, it's good to begin the semester clearly detailing the procedures and expectations for the class. "No surprises," they will think, "that's good." As soon as possible, get them invested by letting them know how important writing is. Tell them this, and show it to them with brief samples of good and bad writing. Also, let them know it is not going to be easy, that writing well is difficult, but that there is a way. "Good," they will think, "I must not be the only one who finds writing a challenge." When you ask someone to write something for you, really write something that is new, original, and unique, you are asking for real communication, for them to share a part of themselves, and that doesn't happen when a person is not engaged and at ease.

Planning for a Successful Semester

To help your students meet their objectives, you need a good plan. But keep in mind what Winston Churchill famously said, "Planning is essential. Plans are useless." You'll find this to be true as you navigate your way through the semester. Making a plan and an assignment sequence based on the desired student outcomes is essential, but you won't be able to follow it precisely. Because things will happen throughout the semester—where you find you need to spend more (or less) time on something than expected, when you decide that one outcome is more important than another, when you realize it's going to take a little something different to move your students forward. These alterations to your plan could be based on your students' work, class discussions, flashes of insight, or current events that you want to incorporate into your classes. Every day you should have a plan, but with contingencies because things don't always happen like you expect.

When you craft your assignment sequence, it's best to start at the end—what do you want your students to be able to do by the end of the semester? If you don't know that, it's impossible to put together a good plan for the semester. Your class goals may vary slightly depending on your school and department, but most schools want students who complete a first-year writing class to write clearly and concisely, show evidence of critical thinking in their writing, be able to summarize and paraphrase other writers, and engage in academic research. My department has been using a research paper rubric (written by yours truly), and all composition students' final research papers are graded with the same rubric. All teachers are helping their students be able to reach these goals, and all new teachers get this rubric before the semester begins so they can see precisely what their students should be able to do at the end of the semester. Here is the rubric:

Thesis/ Argument (15 points)	Paper lacks a clear thesis/ argument or the thesis/ argument does not properly address assignment.	Thesis/ argument is present but needs to be more clear, compelling, or specific.	Thesis/ argument is clear, well-developed, and compelling.
Points Earned	0 – 8	9 – 12	13 – 15
Audience Awareness and Readers' Needs (15 points)	Paper shows limited awareness of the needs of intended audience and/or does not meet the reader's needs for explanation and supporting information.	Paper shows basic awareness of needs of intended audience and meets most, but not all, of the reader's needs for explanation and supporting information.	Paper shows excellent awareness of needs of intended audience and meets the reader's needs for explanation and supporting information.
Points Earned	0 – 8	9 – 12	13 – 15

Academic Research (15 points)	Thesis/argument has not been developed with relevant college-level researched sources.	Thesis/argument is built on ideas or information from researched sources, but these sources are either insufficient or the ideas/information presented from these sources is under-developed.	Thesis/argument has been developed with compelling, relevant, college-level researched sources.
Points Earned	0 – 8	9 – 12	13 – 15
Development of Writer's Ideas (15 points)	The writer fails to provide original ideas and does not build on ideas and information from the research materials. There is not evidence of the writer's critical and creative thinking.	The writer's ideas, including those built on ideas and information from the research materials, are under-developed, insufficiently insightful and valid, and do not show enough evidence of critical and creative thinking.	The writer's ideas, both original ideas and those built on ideas and information from the research materials, are insightful and valid and show evidence of critical and creative thinking.
Points Earned	0 – 8	9 – 12	13 – 15

Structure and Organization (15 points)	Some or all paragraphs contain excessive or unnecessary information or ideas that do not develop the thesis/ argument. Some or all paragraphs are not presented in proper form. Some ideas may be presented in illogical order.	Paragraphs generally focus on subtopics related to the thesis/ argument, do not contain excessive, unnecessary information or ideas, and are adequately formed and linked to each other.	Paragraphs are appropriately formed, focus on subtopics, and all serve to develop the thesis/ argument. They also flow logically from one to the next, with new ideas building on those previously introduced.
Points Earned	0 – 8	9 – 12	13 – 15
Language, Style, Mechanics, and Grammar (15 points)	Language use is too simplistic, technical, informal, and/ or in some other way inap-propriate for the assignment and audience. Word choices are imprecise and/or errone-ous. Sentence structure is very basic or inef-fective. Paper contains exces-sive grammar, punctuation, spelling, and/or other errors.	Language use is appropriate for the assignment and audience. Word choice conveys general meanings but could be more precise. Sen-tence structure is adequate. Paper contains a minimally acceptable level of grammar, punctuation, spelling, and other errors.	Language use is rich, compelling, engaging, and appropriate for the assignment and audience. Word choice precisely conveys meaning. Sentences are structured effectively. Paper is free of grammar, punctuation, spelling, and other errors.
Points Earned	0 – 8	9 – 12	13 – 15

MLA Format (10 points)	The paper does not follow MLA guidelines, source materials are not cited, and paraphrases and quotations are not credited to their sources. Intentional Plagiarism will result in a grade of 0 for the entire paper.	Paper generally follows MLA guidelines, but there are errors citing sources and properly presenting paraphrases and quotations.	Paper follows MLA guidelines. All sources are properly cited, and all paraphrases and quotations are presented correctly.
Points Earned	0 – 8	9 – 12	13 – 15
Total Points and Comments: Grading Scale: A 93-100 A- 90-92 B+ 88-89 B 83-87 B- 80-82 C+ 78-79 C 73-77 C- 70-72 D+ 68-69 D 63-69 D- 60-62 F 59 & below			

Even though I agree with Sun Tzu when he says, "A victorious army first obtains conditions for victory, then seeks to do battle," through trial and error, I have learned it's best to not get too specific with all of the "conditions." For example, this rubric (like all that I use) allows for different ways to meet the goals of the assignment and earn a good grade. There is not a set number of required sources. There is no maximum threshold for grammatical errors. I don't want my students to feel like they are checking boxes when they write a paper. Instead, I want them to know there are countless ways to succeed.

I craft much of my assignment sequence based on the set of goals I have for the research paper, but I don't have a fixed assignment sequence I use every semester. Instead, I lay out (for myself) a very simple plan with key objectives, steps along the path, but not with specific assignments determined (though I have got lots of options for assignments and I am always trying out new ones).

Here is a general outline of what I'll have in mind (with the main objective for each week) when I start a fifteen-week class:

Week 1	Introduce students to the class and each other, start to get them invested in writing, collect some informal, ungraded writing
Week 2	Continue what we've started in Week 1, Photo Essay, assign and introduce Reading #1
Week 3	Discuss Reading #1, discuss student response essays, assign Paper #1, incorporate exercises as needed
Week 4	Peer Review Paper #1, assign and introduce Reading #2, incorporate exercises as needed

Week 5	Paper #1 due for grade, conferences, discuss Reading #2
Week 6	Discuss responses to Reading #2, assign Paper #2
Week 7	Peer Review Paper #2
Week 8	Paper #2 due for grade, assign Paper #3 (Research Paper), hand out and discuss rubric, read over sample Research Papers
Week 9	Library Session 1: Introduction to the Databases
Week 10	Research Proposal due, Library Session 2: Finding Sources
Week 11	Conferences to discuss Paper #3 (outline due at conference)
Week 12	Peer Review Paper #3
Week 13	Conferences
Week 14	Paper #3 due for grade
Week 15	Review/Reflective Exercises

For the first graded paper (rough draft not due until Week 4), the objectives are to sum up an essay (usually "Self-Reliance") and then present an argument about contemporary society that is connected to an idea from Emerson's essay. Sometimes I even tell my students to use one of Emerson's ideas as a "critical lens" to look at something in the world today, but even this feels a little too formal for me. Depending on how well students do on Paper #1, I figure out what they need to do for Paper #2. Maybe more of the same. Maybe a rhetorical analysis. Maybe a personal essay. Maybe we just need to stop and work on grammar and paraphrasing. Maybe we are ready to start working on the research paper.

My goal for the class is to help students develop the skills they need to be strong writers. But I can't just teach "skills" because I also need to get students invested, get them to think as a team, trust me and all the other things I've discussed. While I follow the same pattern of assignments early in the semester, I have fewer and fewer specific assignments in mind as it builds, until we get to the research paper. The reason for this is because the strategies I use to reach my objectives change with each new class and student. I've always got my end goals in sight, getting them ready to write that final paper and then writing it, but I can't just lay out an assignment sequence and expect to follow it. Because everything that happens in the semester affects everything that follows. I don't know what my students will need. They may need help with critical reading. They may need to do only one exercise on using specific examples to support their points, or they may need more. You won't know exactly what your students need until you know who they are and see how they write. Hopefully, you've got a cache of in-class and out-of-class readings, assignments, and exercises you can rely on. If that's not the case, you should ask your fellow teachers for help. Or come up with your own. Again, it's important that you are able to put yourself in the position of the students, figuring out what they want and what they need.

For example, sometimes midsemester, after submitting Paper #2, knowing my students are busy studying for midterms in other classes, I've decided the best thing for them is to watch a video (that is relevant to something we have covered or will cover in class), spend part of a class session working in groups writing the worst Secret Admirer letter imaginable, or write a conversation between their current and past selves. Little exercises like this keep the class moving forward without dragging anyone down (especially me). If you are always on your toes, prepared to make changes, to adapt to things as they happen, it's easier to keep your students engaged.

Starting the Semester

Now that you know how to see yourself, how to present yourself, what to expect from your students (generally), and what you can do to plan the full semester, I am going backwards, in a way, to talk about *starting* the semester and getting your students engaged with writing, with each other, and with you. So far, I have focused on big-picture stuff, for you and the class as a whole. But knowing yourself and the general tendencies of your students is only the start. To effectively teach your students, you need to get to know each one individually. Of course, each student has a different background, learns differently, and responds to different kinds of teaching. Some respond to personal attention, others don't. Some thrive in a structured environment, others flounder. Some learn best when they are interacting with others, others by sitting back and watching. Part of your job is to figure out which students learn in which ways and teach accordingly. You may have to meet with probably twenty or so students at a time, but that does not mean you can't be reaching them in different ways. The class you are teaching has provided you and your students the opportunity to meet. But in a writing class, you can't just focus on the content or teaching "lessons" because they don't all learn the same way.

This means that a good amount of your time and energy the first weeks of the semester needs to be spent getting to know students' individual strengths and weaknesses, likes and dislikes. You won't know how to teach them until you know who they are—not just generally, or hypothetically, but *actually*. It isn't easy getting to know twenty, forty, sixty, eighty students simultaneously, but you need to get inside their heads, every one of them, to know how they think and what they want, to discover how they'll learn. You need to see the world, and especially the class you're teaching, through your students' eyes. This is a challenging task, but if you are a teacher, a writer, and a reader, it's a skill you've been developing for some time. You do this every time you engage in one of these activities, and this is why you are in a position to make a real difference in your students' lives.

How do you discover what each student needs? Sun Tzu says, "Provoke him, to know his patterns of movement." Generally, you do this by throwing interesting questions at them and paying close attention to their answers to figure out their priorities, habits, histories, practices, beliefs, et cetera.

The easiest and most effective way to probe and provoke your students is to get them to write. This should start as soon as possible. On the very first day of class, after I've taken attendance, gone over the syllabus, and answered any questions they have, I don't go around the room and have them introduce themselves: "Yeah, I'm a freshman, too. I haven't decided on a major yet . . ." I mean, why put them on the spot like that, with all that stress, for such a small amount of useless information? Yes, I want to get them comfortable speaking in class, but there's time for that, and better ways to do it.

So on that first day, I don't ask them to speak a word. Instead, I have them write a short letter to me: "Dear Professor Nelson . . ." I'll even write this on the board so they know what to call me and to get them started. Then I'll write some other questions on the board:

- What are your goals for this class?
- Describe a good writing/English class experience you have had. What made it good?
- Describe a bad writing/English class experience you have had. What made it bad?
- What do you like to read?
- What is the best thing you have ever written (this could be a paper for class, a short story or poem, a love letter or break-up letter, a journal entry, etc.)?
- How do you really feel about writing? Please be honest, and if you are not a fan of writing, tell me why . . .
- What else should I know about you as a student or writer?

Sometimes I also ask for their take on some current event they've probably been talking and thinking about— the current sports season, new movies, popular TV shows, campus news. I encourage them to be honest, especially about how they feel about writing. "If you don't like writing," I tell them, "write about that. Write about why you don't like it. I want to know why you don't like it." This can be very liberating for them—allowing them to voice their resistance. I also ask them to write about what they expect their biggest challenge will be over the course of the semester. This can help focus them on overcoming weaknesses right away. Sometimes I add a couple open-ended, mind-opening questions, like: "Pepsi or Coke? The chicken or the egg? Yogurt: friend or foe?" These questions change depending on my mood, the season, and what's going on in the world. Questions like these also keep them from taking me, themselves, or the letter too seriously.

I reserve about twenty minutes at the end of the first class session for this, the same amount of class time it would take to have them all tell you their names and majors, and I'm always surprised by how much I learn from these letters. And this is the best kind of exercise for a composition class, especially early in the semester, because it's simultaneously accomplishing multiple goals—for both me and the students. They are writing—which is always good. I'm gathering information on them, as individuals and as writers. By writing a letter to me, they are opening themselves up to me and my guidance, letting their guards down a bit. And already, on the first day of class, I'm establishing a one-on-one relationship with each of them. Whatever else they get from that first day, they'll know that their voice matters, that I care, and that composition class is going to be different. The time I spend reading these letters is delightful (okay, *enjoyable*), and the benefits are immeasurable. Surprisingly, lots of students will mention their favorite high school English teachers, who changed their lives, who "rocked their worlds" and led them to love to read and write. When I first started asking for this letter, this was a revelation to me—they'd all be sitting there with their blank faces as I went over the syllabus, looking as uninterested as can be, but in these letters was evidence that, simmering beneath the surface, they had real enthusiasm for the class, or at least an interest in being enthusiastic. If you try this, I think you'll find lots of your students are more open to the idea of enjoying composition class than you may have assumed. While they may not be exactly like you, your students are more kindred in spirit than you might think.

When I read over the letters, I do so with a highlighter in my hand, noting funny, interesting comments along with some of those that seem to be more universal, related to writing or otherwise. I'll read these excerpts aloud in class later in the week or at the start of the next week. The students enjoy this, and it helps bring them together when they see they have things in common and see that their classmates are willing to actually reveal things about themselves. They won't get that in other classes, and this helps establish the focus of the class, which is writing, of course, but it's also them—what they think and care about. When they realize that, they immediately get more invested.

To give you an idea of the kinds of responses I get, here are a few from a recent class, all in response to the question "How do you really feel about writing?"

I'm not a fan of writing because I feel like I'm not good at it whatsoever. Also because I feel like I can never get exactly what I want into words that make sense to others.

If I'm being honest I have never been a fan of writing because I don't see myself as an excellent writer so I have to put a lot of work into it. But, I always love the feeling of satisfaction when I submit a paper that I am proud of and receive a good grade.

I've definitely had a lot more negative experiences than positive because I find it's hard for most individuals to truly understand exactly what I am trying to get across in my writing. I had a couple different teachers that would just give me a zero and mark it with "incomplete thoughts" or "spend more time researching" - little things like this! but that's not it at all, I actually put a lot of time into my work "even if it looks sloppy" in the traditional eyes - I have ADD and this is where I struggle so much because I just have so many thoughts coming in a once that it's hard to tie everything together and to really zone down on one thing. like I said above I actually love writing it just very frustrating when I feel very solid about my work - which I always write in a personal style (I can be objective when I need to) and I honestly think it's a good thing a do because it gives readers a chance to hear my voice through my writing if that makes sense.

I like writing when I get into a groove and am inspired, but inspiration rarely strikes. When I do write, I like to write about things I'm passionate about, but I'm at a point in my life where I'm at a crossroads when it comes to life and opinions, so lately it's been hard to draw inspiration from my own ideas as they're pretty "floppy" right now. So I like writing, I just have been struggling with it.

I honestly hate writing. I dislike it because I'm not very good at it. If I want to write a decent paper it takes me forever because I have to make sure I edit it very well with revisions. I just have to work twice as hard as my classmates to produce good writing.

I think I am a pretty good writer. I did pretty well in my high school English cores. I often like writing, because it is a way to share a perspective on a topic and learn something new.

I feel like some writing can be really fun. With some assignments, I catch myself writing pages on end, not really paying attention to how long the paper actual takes. With some other types of paper formats, I sometimes struggle, especially if I learning a new style of writing.

I honestly love writing - I am the type of person that has always had a head full of thoughts/ opinion- however I have had a bit of frustration with English

*classes in the past because of teaching styles and I
simply just am not great about remembering correct
grammar rules and punctuations. teachers would
always tell me in the past that I have great ideas but
they just don't see my main point or they understand
what I was trying to say but need my verbal explanation to see the point I was trying to highlight.*

*I enjoy writing because I feel like I can express my
thoughts and ideas easily. I also tend to see writing
as a way to voice your opinions on various things
without arguments. I also really enjoy being able to
see all your hard work come together in the end. The
one thing that I do not enjoy about writing is the time
it takes me to write my thoughts. I tend to second
guess myself quite a bit, and this takes me more time.
However, I know that this can be fixed!*

As you can see, students are pretty honest, and there is
a wide variety of thoughts and opinions about writing. This
is valuable information for me as we start the semester.

Another exercise I like to use early in the semester to
get to know more about my students and their writing
skills is what I call a Photo Essay. I ask them to choose a
recent photo of themselves and submit a two-page essay
describing the setting and explaining what was going on at
the time, what they were doing, what they were thinking, et
cetera. These often impress me too, and the students enjoy
the assignment, which helps accomplish multiple goals.
Again, it establishes the fact that it's *their* course, that the

class is about them and their writing. It gets them writing, more formally and elaborately than they do in class, but it's still pretty low-stakes, ungraded, not academic yet. Some practical benefits are that I get to learn more about my students: their prom dates, graduations, trips to the Florida Keys. And when I read the essays and study the photos (which they must also submit), I learn their names more quickly, which makes the class move forward faster, and it's easier to ask questions, have conversations, and assign your tasks to students when you can call them by name.

But the bigger benefit of this assignment is that it helps establish the connection between themselves and their writing—the idea that a person's writing is a direct reflection of that person, not something generic that exists apart from the individual. Unfortunately, this generic form of writing seems to be the kind many of them are used to providing for classes. I tell them the papers they write for my class should be papers only *they* could write, which means they are not just providing information, not just passing ideas from others. Some part of what they write for my class has got to be new, unique, original. That's the point of writing, I tell them.

This assignment also provides an opportunity for a good class session, which proceeds like this: They bring their essays and copies of their photos to class, pass just the photos around the class, and then spend eight to ten minutes writing as if they are the student in the photo, either looking at the details and trying to accurately describe the experience, or being as creative as they want to be. A fifty-minute class session allows for three of these quickly written in-class Photo Essays and the opportunity to have some students read aloud what they've written. I'll ask for volunteers, and if I run out of these, I'll go around and grab an interesting-looking photo and ask the people who wrote on that to share what they wrote with the class. Depending on how much time we have, I'll either have the actual subject of the photo read his or her essay or just sum it up in a minute or so. This is a good way to get them started speaking in class (well, mostly just reading aloud, but using their voices), they're writing again, which is always good, they have to be creative to some extent, they get to know each other a bit and actually engage in some pretty high-level thinking, imagining they are someone else—which is exactly the kind of thinking they need to do to develop as writers, readers, thinkers. Of course, they just think they're having fun. Everybody wins.

Sun Tzu also advises that to know your enemy, you should "probe him, to know where he is strong and where he is weak." Strength and weakness can refer to writing strengths and weaknesses, and you'll want to discover these as early as possible (by reading what they have written), but you also need to uncover your students' personalities, their psychology, their demeanors both in the classroom and out of it. You need access to the students' mindsets—both when they are sitting in the classroom with you and when they are alone writing, which is where the real work of the class is done. You need to know all these things about your students to know how to best teach them.

Sometimes early in the semester, I ask my students to write about their favorite food, their "perfect" vacation, the best and worst teacher they've ever had, if they'd rather spend a weekend with their mother or their father. As I have already said, it's usually best, whatever the question, to ask them to explain *why*. If you find you have students who don't want to write about themselves, you can ask them questions like: "Which sport is the toughest (and why)? Do you believe in extraterrestrials (and why)? Is life better in the suburbs (and why)?" The key is to get them to say something, anything, and you can learn from that.

See how they respond to provocative readings. Will they dismiss Roland Barthes' essay "Toys" as much ado about nothing, or will they agree with him that their childhood experiences with toys shaped and socialized them into the people they have become?

See how they respond to good and bad writing. I've had interesting class discussions when I asked my students to compare and contrast a Pablo Neruda love poem with a Hallmark card:

> I don't love you as if you were a rose of salt, topaz,
> or arrow of carnations that propagate fire:
> I love you as one loves certain obscure things,
> secretly, between the shadow and the soul.
>
> I love you as the plant that doesn't bloom but carries
> the light of those flowers, hidden, within itself,
> and thanks to your love the tight aroma that arose
> from the earth lives dimly in my body.

I love you without knowing how, or when, or from where,
I love you directly without problems or pride:
I love you like this because I don't know any other way to love,
except in this form in which I am not nor are you,
so close that your hand upon my chest is mine,
so close that your eyes close with my dreams.

vs.

You and I are connected
in a way that goes beyond romance
beyond friendship—
And it has defied
every explanation except one—
purely and simply
we're soulmates
I can't explain it, I just feel it
It's in the way my spirit lifts
whenever we talk
how the sound of your voice
brings me home in a way
I can't explain.

If they can't see the difference between these in terms
of complexity and the use of language, ask them what they
do see, then help them to see the difference. Pay attention
to everything because everything you observe can be used
to help you teach them more effectively.

As you navigate through the first few weeks of the
semester, along with studying the materials of the class,

you need to be asking yourself questions like: "Does Student A like to speak in class? Does Student B work well in groups? Can Student C follow what I'm saying, or do I need to write this on the board?" You should be constantly provoking and probing your students simply by having them answer questions—about themselves, about readings, about classmates' drafts, about writing both good and bad. You need to listen closely to what they have to say, pay attention to what they do, and figure out what's going on in their minds.

You also need to watch how they interact with each other. You can use this knowledge when you are forming compatible, productive groups and just to see how they interact with other people more generally, which will help you understand how to best communicate with them.

In many ways, the first few weeks of the semester are the easiest—the assignments are short, everyone has energy, no one is complaining about grades. It's important to hold on to that feeling of coasting along as long as you can, because it will get harder. The goals you have for your students will be more rigorous. Your challenges as leader will get more complicated.

Before too much time passes, your students will have to be reading something to prepare for a more formal assignment (these will differ based on your school, department, and personal interests), but throughout the semester, never stop following Sun Tzu's advice to "probe" and "provoke" them. Find out who they are at the start of the semester, but also keep pace with them as they develop. Do this by asking open-ended questions and allowing freedom in their response essays. Throughout the semester, I'll sometimes have my students do fifteen or twenty minutes of writing in class. Even if it feels like I should be using that time to "teach" them something, I believe it helps keep them activated, makes them curious about something, and leads to a discovery of one sort or another. It's time well spent. It is teaching.

Reflective writing is also very valuable for developing writers and a way for you to learn more about them. I ask for these to be submitted in conjunction with submission of drafts, final or otherwise, asking students to reflect on both the content of their papers and the process that produced them. You can ask simple questions like: "What is the best element of this draft? What do think still needs to be developed? What ideas or concepts do you think a reader will need the most help with? If this draft was a meal (or an amusement park ride, or a celebrity), which would it be?" Always remind them that they must explain their answers. This helps because, just like body awareness is one of the keys to longevity and self-awareness is a key to clearer thinking, writing awareness is a key to becoming a better writer.

As often as possible, but especially early in the semester, plan activities that lead to experiences—reading aloud, small group discussions, freewriting (all the things that experienced writers do naturally or out of habit). This helps on many levels, and they'll also learn to see that writing is a process.

Some of the more important experiences your students will have are individual conferences with you. In these conferences (typically fifteen to twenty minutes long and held in lieu of class) you and your students can discuss what they've already written, what they plan to write, and anything else you feel is important to the students' success in the class. I suggest having these conferences in public areas—the conversation-friendly areas of the library or on-campus coffee shop, places people typically meet to have conversations, as opposed to your office, where the impression at least is that you've got the upper hand. I like to schedule my first one approximately a month into the semester, after they have submitted the first graded assignment. We discuss that paper, and I also just ask them, "How is class going? How is the semester going? How is life treating you?" This helps me learn more about them and helps establish in their minds that I care about their success in the class.

It also allows me to discover more about what is going on in the class. Sun Tzu says, "One who does not use local guides cannot take advantage of the ground," and our students are our "local guides." This applies to both stronger and weaker students. Use conferences to ask them how they think the class is going, what they have made of the assignments and readings to date. Even if you believe an assignment has worked in the past, don't assume it is working again. Find out. Ask for concerns or complaints about the class and listen closely. There may be improvements you can make. If possible, schedule some time between conferences so you can absorb your students' input and make notes to yourself about changes you may need to make.

The semester is long, but it goes by quickly, and you've got a lot of ground to cover, but your main goal for these first weeks of class is to get to know your students, introduce them to each other, help them begin to see themselves as a group, and gain their trust. The more questions they answer, the better you'll get to know them. The more they learn about each other, the closer they'll feel. The more they write, the better they'll write. The more times they write without feeling like they are being controlled, the more invested they'll become in the writing they do.

Uniting the Class

Sun Tzu says, "When the men are united, the brave cannot advance alone; the cowardly cannot retreat alone." Often the hardest thing about forming a group is getting everyone in the same room at the same time. Luckily for you, the administration of the school has done this important work for you. You'll walk into the classroom on day one, and there they'll all be, sitting shoulder to shoulder, gazing up at you. Most times, a class begins as a series of individuals—who may not know each other at all. They won't be able to accomplish as much if they stay that way, so part of your job is to unite them. Not only will this make your job easier, it will help both the strongest and the weakest students thrive. Remember that this is a semester-long battle for Good Writing, and you are responsible for every student in the class. It's important you work individually with students at times, and you will, because each student will need his or her own unique type of instruction, but there is simply not enough time to focus exclusively on that.

Most classes run about fifteen weeks. If you're teaching in an accelerated format, you may have only six or eight weeks. Either way, your goal should be to have them thinking of themselves as a group after no more than one-fifth of the way through the course. You can't rush it or force it, but you've got to be subtly moving them to think of themselves that way from the start. Maybe you haven't thought of yourself as inspirational, a politician, a galvanizer of troops, but you don't have to be because it's simple human nature to want to belong. As Abraham Maslow explained in his Hierarchy of Needs, after our essential (physiological and safety) needs are met, we want our social needs met, as explained in this pyramid:

SELF-
ACTUALIZATION:
Achieving one's full
potential, including
creative activities

ESTEEM NEEDS:
Prestige and feeling of accomplishment

BELONGINGNESS AND LOVE NEEDS:
Intimate Relationships, Friends

SAFETY NEEDS:
Security, Safety

PHYSIOLOGICAL NEEDS:
Food, Water, Warmth, Rest

https://www.simplypsychology.org/maslow.html

As far as physiological needs go, let's assume your students are fed, clothed, and that the classroom is reasonably comfortable. Their safety needs are not just physical,

but psychological, and that's why it's important to demon-
strate your generosity, benevolence, and fair-mindedness.
Once you've established this, you can begin uniting them.
The key is to have a common goal (embracing The Way
and becoming better writers) and common identity based
on that goal.

One key to bonding a group of strangers is to get them
to *all* work together. This is important, because as Sun
Tzu says, "One who knows how to unite upper and lower
ranks in purpose will be victorious." That means you need
to get your stronger students to work with the weaker
ones, to understand that it is their responsibility to help
each other, to not leave anyone behind. So instead of some
students reaching the class goals and others foundering,
they will all be moving towards reaching the goals. Of
course, there will be stragglers, and you will need to give
those students the extra individual attention they need,
but this is much easier once you've got the group working
properly because the group will continue to move forward
on its own (with just a little prodding and pointing from
you) and the stragglers will want to do the work to rejoin
the group.

It is possible that your students stay distinct and separate from each other the whole semester and still improve.
It's also true that you could leave them all on their own for
fifteen weeks, giving them only a set of assignments and
deadlines, and they could make some progress that way
too. But their achievements in either of these scenarios
would be far less and far less satisfying than what they
can do under the guidance of a strong leader and with

everyone in the class working together. And when they are working together, your job is easier.

How do you get the more skilled, experienced, and ambitious students to want to help the others, who may not only give the impression they don't want help, but that they don't care about improving? Well, hopefully they will adopt your generous, empathetic attitude. Second, you need to show them that teaching something to someone else, explaining it, is one of the best ways to learn. Just like you learn more about writing through teaching, your students will learn by helping each other. This is doubly important because it also means no students are sacrificing themselves for the others. No one is holding anyone else back. Your students will understand things better when they view them from other perspectives. Your students will find it's often easier to come up with creative solutions when solving problems for others, as opposed to themselves. Your students will come into the class with different skills, appreciation for writing, good and bad habits, et cetera. Your challenge is to teach the class in a way that they all improve. Don't let your strongest writers coast through the semester. For writers, the whole realm of human experience and all the various ways to use language are available for investigation. Tell your students that it is *always* possible to become a better writer (and no one ever regrets it).

Can I be more practical about how to establish this group identity and draw from this endless well of cooperation? Yes, and practically the first thing to do is to have your students see each other—so arrange their seats to be facing each other as often as is possible. I mean, it's hard to get to know people and have empathy for them if all you see is their backs, or if you don't see them at all, which is the case in the typical classroom configuration. Next, you can begin to unite the class the ways you'd unite any sort of group—by getting them invested in reaching their common goal, and by helping them get to know some details of each other's lives. You don't need them all to become friends, and there may be students who don't particularly like each other, but they can still work together, in the classroom at least. One way to help them bond is to show them what they have in common and make that more important than what they don't. As I have already explained, reading excerpts from their first-day letters is an easy and effective way to do this.

Team-building exercises are important at the beginning of the semester. I like to start small, then expand. For example (the idea that this is a team-building exercise started as kind of a joke I'd make, but it's true), on the first day of class, I hand out a calendar of the upcoming three or four weeks. Because this calendar only takes up half a page, I can fit two copies on a single sheet of paper. I give one to every other student and ask them to fold it, tear it in half, and share with the person sitting next to them. It's such an easy task, but you wouldn't believe how many students struggle with this. It's not because it's hard to do, but because they feel like they've got someone watching them, a *stranger*. After the folds and tears (of varying success—I usually bring a few extras for exceptionally bad tears), whether the person is the giver or the receiver, they have bonded with another student, sometimes showing off a strength, but more often revealing a bit of weakness, or seeing it in another student. This helps break down barriers.

Another exercise I've used with success early in the semester, usually the second day of the semester, is an exploration of what good writing is. Class proceeds like this: I write the question on the board: What is good writing? I tell them to think about all kinds of writing, not just academic writing. I tell them to think about novels, poetry, love letters, articles, jokes, blogs, posts, anything that can be written. The first step is to have students freewrite (the only rule: don't stop writing) on the topic for about ten minutes. I ask for sample responses and write some of these on the board. Then I break the class into small groups and give them ten more minutes to come up with an all-encompassing definition of "good writing" (small groups work best on tasks like this that are challenging, but attainable). Each group then writes their definition on the board, and as a class, we discuss further. The students forge bonds as they work in the groups, and the class discussion helps show them they're all in the same boat, as it were. It also establishes (in their own words, as a product of their own thinking) the goals for the class: Good Writing! I also like this exercise because it's the kind you don't quite reach the end of. No group has ever arrived at a definitive, all-encompassing answer to the question. This session also gives me a sense of what they value in writing, what they've been taught, and it gives me an opportunity to discuss what I think is important. Of course, it's also a great exercise in writing, because coming up with a definition for "good writing" is a challenge. Usually, the day after this exercise, I will bring in a "final answer" to the question based on their definitions, something like: Good writing is on a topic and in a style appropriate for the intended audience, is engaging and interesting, employs language well, is concise, stays focused, develops ideas, is free of distracting errors, and leaves the reader with knowledge or insight into an idea, emotion, situation, et cetera. If we all agree on this, we can refer to it later in the semester. I can even use it when I hand back graded papers or for reflective exercises, asking them how well they think their work measures up.

Other team-building exercises are the in-class component of the Photo Essay, collaborative writings, and group work. Full-class discussions with lively, engaged students are great, but these rarely happen spontaneously. You need to train your students to be active, invested participants. Time spent freewriting or engaged in small groups typically leads to better full-class discussions because the students are warmed up, have been thinking in a safe, comfortable environment, and all have something to contribute, even if it's just posing a question or admitting they are confused. I have rarely had successful full-class discussions at the very start of a class period, probably because my students haven't been thinking excitedly about the day's lesson like I have. I have learned that part of my job at the start of each session is to recalibrate them for class, activate them for the day's work.

A full-class discussion is a great way to explore ideas and team strength and rapport. However, at times you will surely encounter the dreaded silent classroom. While all prolonged silences make me uncomfortable, not all silences are the same, and as a teacher, you need to know the difference between "productive silence" and disengagement or a lull in thinking. Productive silence is just what it sounds like: quiet time that is being used for thinking. You'll know it is productive if, at the end of it, someone (not you) says something that moves the class discussion in a good direction. Unfortunately, you won't know if it is productive until it's over. But if you have a class discussion that does not progress, there are a few possible reasons: the reading you had them do is too hard, the questions you are asking are not clear enough, the students don't care about the questions or answers, or the students simply haven't done the work to prepare. There may be other kinds of classroom dynamics in play, making students uncomfortable. Sometimes you can wait it out and will be rewarded, but other times you'll need to change direction and activate them somehow, maybe by having them do some writing (alone or in groups), answering questions, posing questions, or re-reading something. What you don't want to do is go through a whole class session trying to have a class discussion and get no input from your students. If, for whatever reason, they are not going to interact, you are better off lecturing to them, or, if you don't like that word, explaining things to them. You can often cover more ground that way and leave time for something else, perhaps asking them to write answers to questions about the lecture you just gave, or ask questions: what else do they need to know? Even if they are all being quiet, I promise you some of them are having interesting thoughts that they will share and that you can use to make the class better.

To get your students united, you've got to act like a coach, psychologist, cheerleader, and more. It's important, because as Sun Tzu says, "Square shapes are still, but round shapes roll." You need your students to be round so they can roll and make progress. This applies to individual students, but also to the lot of them as a group. You want them to roll forward together, improve together, but to make that happen, you need to smooth out their rough edges, the things that may hold back their working together: their different histories, attitudes, lifestyles, values, interests, and appearances. While these differences can add energy to the classroom, and understanding different perspectives is integral to the course, on some levels, they've got to forget about their differences. You can help make this happen by rubbing them together a little bit to break off these sharp edges, softening them up, smoothing them out. By having them work together in a safe environment, you lead them to accept each other on some level, at least for the duration of the course. And always let them hear you thinking, "You're all in this together. It's the writing that matters!" Get them to believe this, and then, instead of a bucket of blocks, you'll have a bucket of balls, and when you tip them out in the right direction, you can just let them go, watch them build steam, gain momentum, and learn to write!

Luring Them to the Battlefield

The next key is luring your students to the battlefield, the place you and your students meet. Sun Tzu called it the battlefield because he was writing about war. For us, it's something different. It's not the classroom exactly; it's more of a metaphysical meeting place—where your thoughts and ideas on writing interact with theirs, where the definitions, understandings, practices, and habits of Good Writing can overthrow the Bad. Of course, many students, even those who know they need to improve as writers, will come into the semester entrenched in their ideas and attitudes about writing, uninterested in change. College students also want to think they are in control, want to move beyond the oversight and rules of high school and make their own decisions. The key is to get students to *want* to approach the battlefield. Sometimes you can do this with tricks, but more generally, you'll do it with promises of personal growth and gain (explicitly stated only when necessary). Different students need to be lured in different ways, and you'll have to figure these out. But one way or another, you've got to get them to the battlefield, because this is the only place you use the forces of Good Writing to supplant the Bad. The battlefield is where you'll be in control, where you'll have the advantage, and where they begin to see the light, appreciate Writing as The Way.

A simple behavioral rule to remember is that the best motivation is intrinsic, doing something because one *wants* to do it; not extrinsic, doing something because one *has* to do it, for either a reward or because someone else wants it done. I suppose that's obvious, but there's more to it than that. I have read that not only is intrinsic motivation more powerful, it's been found that too much extrinsic motivation, no matter what the activity, even something a person likes to do, undermines one's intrinsic motivation. In other words, the more someone else wants you to do something, the less motivated you are to do it on your own. So whatever you decide to have your students focus on, remember that the key is to get them to *want* to write, for *their* benefit, not for rewards you dangle in front of them.

Another way to keep them motivated is through their natural curiosity. They may not always look like it, but they are curious. Take advantage of that to keep them invested. They also like to be challenged. Again, your students may not appear that way, but it's true. Remember the rants from the students about their crummy composition teacher? They had a number of issues with him, but one of the big ones was that they weren't being challenged. Everyone knows that the way to learn is by overcoming challenges. Of course, we don't want everything in life to be a challenge—we like rituals, routines, and sometimes to relax. But the only way to grow is by overcoming a challenge, and that's what your students are in college for.

But challenging your students is tricky because you can only do so after they've gotten invested. You can't do it from day one, like maybe a coach of a sports team can. That's a different dynamic. Athletes are on teams by choice. Composition class is required. But the coach/athlete relationship is similar in that an athlete who wants to improve, and trusts his or her coach, will pay close attention to what the coach says, will follow directions and work hard.

One way to facilitate student engagement is to think of yourself as the "author" of the class, with your students your readers. An author's goal is to "entrance" readers—pull them in so it feels like time stops and nothing else matters. As author of the classes you are teaching, you need to draw your students in, get them invested, get them to care to the point that they'll hold on, even when it gets hard, even when it may be frustrating. To make this work, you'll need to remember that one goal most readers have is to expend as little energy as possible, or, if it becomes clear that isn't possible, be confident that the energy spent will pay off. Your students are typically not going to come to class thinking, "I really want to spend some energy on composition class today!" You need to lead them to places where they've got no choice but to engage with the materials and be willing to put in effort when the task calls for it.

Earlier, I talked about some qualities of your typical composition students, that is, they 1) resist complexity, 2) take the easiest path provided to them, 3) resist authority, and 4) are often nervous and anxious. What this means is that they'll hold back and stay on safe ground whenever possible. The assignments you give them must get them to venture forward from that safe ground. Sometimes you can get them to amble onto the battlefield with no idea that that is where they are headed. But this may only work for a short time. It is better if you can entice them so they *want* to be there, because then they are more likely to stay. Either way, it's important they are not "fortified," that is, you need to get them to drop their weapons and resistance, open their hearts and minds. Ideally, they'll come with their hands up, ready to forget all the Bad Writing practices they've acquired over the years, mumbling, "Teach me, Master. The only thing I know is that I am ignorant." But even if this isn't the case, you need them to be vulnerable. Not because you are going to squash them, but because you're going to *help* them, invite them to come over to your side, become *your* soldiers, with all the rights and privileges they deserve. You are going to swoop in with the forces of Good Writing to show them how they can strengthen their hearts, sharpen their minds, entertain hopes like they'd never imagined.

I like to think of it as luring them to the edge of a pit, then tricking them into throwing themselves, or some part of themselves, into the pit. Inevitably, they'll feel compelled to work their way back out, compelled to find the right words, because once one's self is invested, it's not just work to be done, it *matters*, it is *meaningful*.

For example, when my students first read Emerson's "Self-Reliance," they nod along when he says: be yourself, don't conform, this will bring you peace. "Of course," they say. "It all makes perfect sense." But while it's not a bad thing to have faith in one's self, if it were true, we could all accomplish *whatever* we wanted; in our current states, we'd all be miserable, underachieving failures, myself included, because I really wanted to be an adored novelist by this point in my life, after winning a gold medal in the Olympic 10,000 meters. But as my students continue to talk, think, and write about Emerson's argument or the others on the self that follow, they inevitably question some of the things they value: religion, family, education. Clothes, cars, music. "How does all that fit in?" they wonder. "Am I really self-reliant? Should I be? Is it possible? Am I doing all I can in this life to satisfy myself? Or would that be selfish? Isn't it sometimes better to be a part of a group? Am I supposed to isolate myself?" The kind of writing prompts you can create based on these kinds of topics are great—your students will need to read and sum up a challenging essay, properly present paraphrase and quotations, and then say something else beyond that—something they care about (or will realize they care about when they begin to write). This is how you can get them invested.

Sun Tzu even says, referring to the opposition in this case, "If they are angry, disturb them." So another way to get them invested is to get them emotionally involved, even if it means making them angry. Now, you never want them to be angry with you, but anger in general is not always a bad thing. People do things in fights they wouldn't expect of themselves, and that's what you want your students to do—things they haven't done before. The key is to use that energy they've got stored up, the ability to be angry, something we all have, to produce thinking and writing for the good. For example, having them read something like Paulo Freire's "The Banking Concept of Education" will get them angry at their educations. Reading about the media's unrealistic portrayal of bodies, they'll get angry at the media. They can get angry about politics, the environment, sexism, some of the rules on campus, et cetera. They can get angry at Nietzsche or maybe even Emerson. The list of things people can get angry at is unlimited, and this can be a great way to generate energy.

When you are luring students in, it's important to be patient, because as Sun Tzu says, "Those skilled in warfare make themselves invincible and then wait for the enemy to become vulnerable." If you are truly on the side of The Way, your position will be invincible, and students opposed in any way will reveal themselves eventually. Your job is to plan and prepare, plan and prepare, and wait.

Of course, the semester goes by quickly, so you also need to get things moving. The right kind of writing prompts can speed up the process. My advice when giving a prompt is to not be too prescriptive. Point them towards a goal but give them a choice in how to get there. Steer them towards doing some things well, but also give them space to make mistakes. Now I'm not saying lead them directly into making specific mistakes; instead, direct their energy into places they are likely to make their own. Then, later, you can point these out and redirect their energy. For example, when I have my students write their initial (ungraded) response to Emerson's "Self-Reliance" the assignment sheet looks like this:

- -

Response to "Self Reliance"

For this exercise, you need to write a 2-3 page (typed) response to Emerson's "Self-Reliance."

Your first objective is to accurately sum up his argument by answering some or all of the following questions:

How does Emerson define self-reliance?
According to Emerson, why is it difficult to be self-reliant?
What are the benefits of being self-reliant?
What are the consequences of *not* being self-reliant?

Your second objective is to argue whether or not Emerson's ideas on self-reliance are valid or not. Do you agree with him? Why or why not? (your answer may be a combination of agreement and disagreement). To successfully answer this question, you need to go beyond simply stating your opinion and explain your position. The best way to do this is to look beyond the essay and provide specific examples that support your position (examples from your own life or things you've observed).

Be sure to include evidence from the text to support your points. If you include direct quotations, present them like this:

Emerson says, "Envy is ignorance" (2).

You also need to choose two passages from the essay to discuss in class. It may be a passage you think works well or one that confuses you. Either way, it should be a passage that you feel is worthy of class discussion.

As you read, be sure to take notes, which may include questions, comments, observations, and definitions of words you've looked up. This is a challenging essay, so please plan your time accordingly.

- -

This seems very straightforward to me. There are clear objectives, but also plenty of freedom. The typical student will do some things well, but also make mistakes, from simply presenting quotations wrong (even though I spell out exactly how I want them to do it) and other technical errors, to completely misreading Emerson's argument or not going beyond a simple summary of his main ideas, or simply saying, "I agree with Emerson that self-reliance is the key to one's best life because it is the key." Giving them the freedom to make these kinds of mistakes leads to interesting discussion and forces everyone in the class to look more closely at both "Self-Reliance" and the ways they've responded.

On the day this response is due, I arrange the seats in the room so everyone is facing each other. If the tables and chairs in my classroom don't move, I still have everyone move to the perimeter of the room and face each other. Then we go around the room with students reading one of the quotes they have selected (with the rest of us reading along on our copies), and starting the discussion on it. If they don't start talking about the quote (though most of them do), I'll ask: "Why did you choose that quote? What do you think he means? How does this idea relate to our lives in society today?" This is a great way to get everyone to contribute to class discussion early in the semester, even if it's just by them reading their chosen passage. By letting them choose the sections of the essay to discuss, it reinforces the idea that much of the class is dependent on them, that their participation is essential. And for you, well, you've got no preparation at all for this class session. Assuming you've done the reading, you just sit, listen, and lead the discussion. Sometimes at the end of class, if there are key parts of the essay I want to be sure to discuss, I'll go over them, but that's it. An easy class session. But very productive!

Writing off topic is another kind of mistake I "encourage." I let my students get carried away sometimes by giving them some freedom when they write, especially early in the semester, early in a draft, or with response essays (usually written as an initial response to a reading and as a prelude to a more formal (graded) paper). Two good things can come from this: Students get carried away to interesting, unexpected topics, to ideas that are worth developing for that assignment or another. And if students simply just go off topic and don't end up anyplace interesting or relevant, I can show them why what they have written is distracting, how it obscures meaning, how it may confuse the reader, et cetera. A big part of writing is not only producing words, but knowing which to keep and which to throw away. If one of the sample responses we read goes astray, we discuss it and then agree it's best to cut out the parts of the paper that are not on topic. If this happens, I like to share a quote from Isaac Bashevis Singer, who said, "The wastebasket is a writer's best friend."

As Sun Tzu says, "Those skilled in warfare establish positions that make them invincible and do not miss opportunities to attack the enemy." In this case, as usual, the enemy is Bad Writing, whether it comes in the form of bad organization, content, clarity, style, grammar, whatever. In terms of the writing process, I've found it's best to have my students focus on ideas first, finding something to say, before moving on to structure, mechanics, language, et cetera. Once they've got something meaningful written down (that is, something that has meaning for them), they will pay more attention, making sure the structure, mechanics, language, et cetera, aren't getting in the way of obscuring that meaning. But when they make mistakes, big or small (and trust me, they will all make mistakes with everything they write), you've reached the all-important "teaching moment," which you must learn to recognize and take advantage of.

So, to reiterate, you need to make a sound plan, get a feeling for your students, their habits, strengths, and weaknesses. You can watch them closely by having them write about something they care about. Of course, you'll want to point out what they've done well and tell them to continue, and just as importantly, you need to wait for them to err and then "attack." But always remember you are "attacking" the error as a means of "rescuing" the student, bringing him or her over to your side, never to hurt the student.

At the start of a discussion of a recently completed reading, and when discussing the elements of writing or a sample work, the Socratic method of questions and more questions and eventually some answers encourages participation and critical thinking, helps make students aware of what they know and what they don't know, and allows them to not only discover answers to your questions but create new questions of their own. Sometimes these question-and-answer sessions lead exactly where I hope they will (for example, a student saying, "Oh, that's what you mean by 'Show, don't Tell'"). Other times, they lead in completely unexpected directions and discoveries about writing or the content of the piece. Either way, as you plan these sessions, remember that most students in composition class are typically not well versed in the discourse of analysis—so asking vague, open-ended questions ("What did you think about that? How do you like it?") will lead to vague, open-ended answers. You will usually want to ask very specific questions and ask for specific answers and explanations.

For example, after I have my students read Annie Dillard's "Living Like Weasels," an essay I love both for the style and the ideas, I'll have them write answers to these questions:

What qualities in the weasel does Dillard appreciate?

What does Dillard learn from her encounter with the weasel?

According to Dillard, in what ways do weasels live their lives differently than people do?

Do you think it is possible to live life like (according to Dillard) weasels do?

Dillard argues that people would be better off if they lived more like weasels. What animal do you think people should model their lives (behaviors, attitudes, et cetera) after? Why?

Other times, the best questions are the ones you don't know the answer to or can't answer, like "Should people care about how they will be remembered, or if they will be remembered fifty years after they have died?" I don't know the answer to that. Maybe they should. Or maybe it'll prevent them from living life to the fullest. You've got to be ready for anything when it comes to these discussions, but it's still important that you prepare well. Have your questions written down. As I have already said, having your students write about the subject before you begin to discuss ensures they'll have something to say, and small-group discussions before full-class discussions serve the same purpose. A full-class discussion may lead the class to interesting ideas you have not even considered. That is great. But remember, it is your job to keep the discussion focused. No matter how many interesting tangents you end up exploring, you want to reach your objectives by the end of the session. And this method, besides bringing your students to a better understanding of the material at hand, will help show them the value of asking questions and searching for answers, essential skills for writers.

When having question-and-answer sessions, while it's helpful to use your more advanced students to serve as examples/models, you also need to resist relying on them too heavily. This is sometimes difficult—sometimes without even realizing it, you'll find yourself calling on the same old reliable students, just to keep things moving. But there are often students sitting in class who can provide even better responses. You need to find them. It's also a good practice for all your students to get comfortable speaking in class, so you should try to involve everyone. I know some teachers keep track of this as a way to encourage discussion and award points for class participation, but I prefer to let things develop more organically. It's also true that some students learn better when they don't have to speak—when they can just sit back and listen, they absorb more that way. It's your job to figure all this out. Sometimes I'll ask the quieter students directly, calling them by their names, especially if I think they have something to say based on a previous class discussion, or piece of writing, or sometimes just a look in the eyes. Most students *do* have something to say, and sometimes what they say is even better than what you could have imagined. Sometimes they have answers, but even when they don't, it can lead to a positive outcome.

For example, recently, I called on a student after we had just read the opening paragraph of "Self-Reliance" together as a way of introducing them to his style and getting some context before they read the whole thing. I asked her what she thought he meant when he wrote that one should "learn to detect and watch that gleam of light which flashes across his mind from within, more than the luster of the firmament of bards and sages." She fumbled and mumbled a bit, and then just said, "I know what I want to say, but I just can't find the words."

"Precisely," I said. "And this is why we practice writing, this is why it matters, so we can find the words to say what we want to say, to say what we feel."

I didn't come out and tell them writing was The Way. I've never used that phrase in class, but I hope she could see that it is The Way. I hope they all could see it.

Another thing Sun Tzu says is "One who is prepared and waits for the unprepared will be victorious." Obviously, your preparation is only half of this equation. You also need your students to be unprepared. This doesn't mean they will be unprepared for class; it means they will not be prepared for the "battles" you've got planned. They will not have it "all figured out." For example, if we've just read "Self-Reliance" and my students have been inspired to be more self-reliant, think for themselves, be deliberate about achieving their own success, they might expect that the class may continue to deliver that same message. So I might assign something from the opposite point of view, a short article that says the current generation is too self-centered, or lacks empathy, or grit, all because society and their parents have been telling them all along how great they are and to believe in themselves and that they can do whatever they put their minds to—Emerson's ideas taken too far. Now they will not only be a little confused about whether or not self-reliance is a good thing, they've got to look at themselves and either admit the deficiencies described in the articles or defend themselves and explain why the article is inaccurate. So, somewhat paradoxically, you've got to prepare them to be unprepared, mislead them in a way, leading them to situations where you can most easily and efficiently teach them.

Sun Tzu also says, "The one who first occupies the battlefield awaiting the enemy is at ease." This doesn't mean you need to be the first one to arrive in the class-room each day. Sometimes I like to be there first, but other times I arrive closer to the starting time, same as them, unpacking my bag after some of them have already begun to have their conversations (sadly this is getting less common with more cell phone activity, but it still happens sometimes). Though it's important to be available, this way it feels more like their classroom, or our classroom, but not mine. I think if you are always sitting there at the desk in the front of the room when they walk in, they'll feel like they're walking into *your* class, like you're a judge in his or her courtroom, but that's not the attitude you want to convey. And I usually have my best conversations with students after class, when I'm not thinking about what we need to accomplish in the next hour.

While you won't know exactly what will happen in the classroom each day for each session, same as when you plan for the semester, you should have a clear end goal, or set of goals, in mind. Work backwards towards that. Ask yourself: "What should my students be able to do after completing class today? Is it to better understand an essay they've just read, an idea you have discussed, some part of the writing process, the value of an introduction, the difference between stating an opinion and presenting an argument, how to detect a writer's bias, how to make one's self credible?" Whatever it is, be sure everything is working towards that goal in one way or another. When you get there first and set that goal, you are in a better position to help them arrive.

I view the goals for a composition class as very ambitious. Changing the way people think and communicate are no small matters. Students must learn, grow, and develop, and it's a long road from Point A to Point B. Students need to be able to do things they have never done before. But I've never understood why some composition teachers think it is a good strategy to confound their students right away, disorient them with difficult readings, then slowly help them learn to reorient themselves. This is like throwing someone who does not know how to swim into deep water. It may not be the worst way to proceed (I suppose never getting in the water would be worse), but I don't think it's the best. Even though Sun Tzu says when they are "confused" you should "take them," I don't think you ever want your students to be genuinely confused with the materials you give them. For example, I believe starting them off with something like Derrida at the start of the semester is a sure way to frustrate them. Here's a small sample of a text used by some composition teachers for a freshman writing class:

I do not teach truth as such; I do not transform myself into a diaphanous mouthpiece of eternal pedagogy: I settle accounts, however I can, on a certain number of problems; with you and with me or me, and through you, me and me, with a certain number of authorities represented here. I understand that the place I am now occupying will not be left out of the exhibit or withdrawn from the scene. Nor do I intend to withhold even that which I shall call, to save time, an autobiographical demonstration, although I must ask you to shift its sense a little and to listen to it with another ear. I wish to take a certain pleasure in this, so that you may learn this pleasure from me.

(The Ear of the Other: Otobiography, Transference, Translation: Texts and Discussions with Jacques Derrida)

Now I realize one of the goals of a composition class is to teach your students to make sense of complex ideas, but immersing them in something like this—something that they can't relate to or even begin to ground in their reality, even if you do pull their heads back up out of the water—will result initially in confusion, possibly anger, and then frustration. And when students get frustrated and they can see their teacher's fingerprints all over their frustration, they are very likely to turn against the teacher. Students in a class like this may pay close attention, but that's because they think the teacher has all the answers, and most of them will spend the semester trying to figure out what the teacher wants them to say or do. They will see the teacher as the jailer with the key.

Even if the material is appropriate, you don't want your students to view you, and not themselves, as the source of the answers. For example, if you taught a class on Shakespeare and someone asked the students what they learned, you wouldn't want them to say, "I learned *what* to think about Shakespeare." You'd want them to say, "I learned *how* to think about Shakespeare." I mention this example because recently I met with an alumnus of the university I teach at, who is currently a high school English teacher, and he was asking if some others in the English department were still around. He particularly remembered one teacher, and he said, "Most of what he said was way over my head, but he really knew his stuff!" He was saying this to be complimentary. And I knew the teacher he was talking about, and yeah, he did know his stuff, but is that what he taught them, what *he* knew? I suppose it is different for other classes, but for a composition class, the best teacher is one whose teaching almost nullifies the need for a teacher. The goal is to get students to be independent, resourceful, and creative: to be writers.

And this fits with Sun Tzu's advice to "seize what he values (so) he will do what you wish." So instead of giving students the toughest readings and assignments at the start of the semester, I've found a better plan is to craft an assignment sequence that begins with personal experiences, *then* has them respond to other writers' ideas, *then* has them tackle the most challenging readings and make connections between multiple ideas and their own and engage in high-level analysis. This is how I "lure" them in.

And what do your students value? More than grades, family, friends, their cell phones, or favorite sports teams, or TV shows? They value themselves, of course. They all care a great deal about themselves, and you should use that to your advantage. Now before I go on, I want to make it clear that this is not a criticism. It is a natural, inevitable human experience to care about one's self. It is necessary for survival, for success. We all care about ourselves. Of course, it's not the same because we've experienced more than our students have, learned a few more lessons, can see the big picture, and we are also different because we are composition teachers—some of the most generous souls to walk the earth, spending our time and energy making the world a better place.

But do you remember what it was like when you were a freshman in college? How much you thought about yourself? How much you liked or disliked yourself? How smart or not you thought you were? How good-looking and likable? Do you remember how much you cared about all of that? Well, that's what your students are going through. Hopefully, one of the results of your class, of college in general, will be outgrowing this, maturing. But that won't happen in one semester, so the question for us is how do we best teach them while they are in this state?

Sun Tzu says, "Those skilled in moving the enemy use formation to which the enemy must respond. They offer bait that the enemy must take, manipulating the enemy to move while they wait in ambush." For our purposes, the students themselves, or some aspect of themselves, serve as the irresistible bait. The key is to get them writing about themselves, or about topics that matter to them. Don't make the mistake of thinking your students should be interested in the same things you are. Sure, you can focus a writing class on something you believe is important: the environment, education, politics, poverty, literacy, sexism. But trying to get all your students to care about the things you care most about is simply going to end up frustrating you. You can't always get people to care about what you care about, just like others can't get you to care about what they care about. Maybe your students care about hunting or NASCAR or music or religion or conspiracy theories. Let them. At least let them connect what they care about to the topic of the class. Students will write better, at all stages of the process, if they are invested in the topic. And even if you are persuasive, engaging, charming, and brilliant enough that all your students *do* end up caring about the things you want them to care about, I still say it's a dereliction of duty because the energy spent getting those students to care about whatever topic you've gotten them to care about could have been spent teaching them more about writing. The goal of the class is not to show them *what* to care about, *what* to argue for or against, but to show them *how* to use writing to better understand things so they can figure out what *they* care about and then argue for or against that.

Of course, I am not proposing you let them write about themselves all semester, or have too much control over the reading and writing they do. I'm saying lead them (not tell them) to write about things they can relate to personally. When they write me their letters on day one of class, a lot of them say they struggle with writing when they are "forced" to write about a topic they are not interested in. My advice to them, only partly serious, is to get interested in whatever topic has been assigned. What they write about in a lot of classes is out of their control, but you can put them in control, to an extent, in your class and make it easy for them to care about what they write by assigning challenging, important readings and asking them to connect these ideas to topics they can relate to and get interested in. For example, after they read Plato's "Allegory of the Cave," they can think (and write) about the extents to which we are all sheltered from reality. After reading Mihaly Csikszentmihalyi's "What is the Self?" they can try to discover what forces have shaped them into the people they are.

Though my readings change most every semester, I steer all my composition classes to focus on the idea of "the self" in one way or another. Students come in thinking there is no way to stretch that topic more than a few weeks—by the end of the semester, they see we've only been able to scratch the surface, and that years of reading and writing on the topic will still only be scratching the surface. Some of my favorites beyond those I have already mentioned are Aristotle's "The Aim of Man," Nietzsche's "Morality as Anti-Nature," Susan Engel's "Then and Now: Constructing a Self Through the Past," Roy F. Baumeister's "The Self and Society." Sometimes my classes will read something longer, like Viktor Frankl's "Man's Search for Meaning." But I like to assign the shorter works because then they get exposed to more ideas. And I believe these are the best kinds of readings for a composition class—because they challenge students but also give them the opportunity to connect personally to the ideas presented. And I don't get bored with them. I have spent years teaching these same essays, and the class discussions and valid topics students write about (response papers and research topics) related to these are nearly infinite.

One mistake you don't want to encourage is allowing them to include biographical information on the writers in their responses. I learned this the hard way. I used to give background information on Emerson, telling them that some people would cross the street if they saw him coming towards them because "Self-Reliance" asked people to question organized religion. I'd tell them that the father of super-atheist Nietzsche was a minister. I did this hoping they would get a little more interested in reading these works and understand them a little better if they had some context, saw the authors as real people. But then I'd get responses full of biographical information, what I'd said in class and sometimes more. All completely useless.

So now I come right out and tell my students that I *used to* give longer introductions to our readings, with biographical information on the authors, but I stopped because too many students would just repeat it all back to me. I tell them they may be taking classes where the key to success is to listen closely to what their teacher says and then restate it, but that is not the case for this class. I tell them I want to see what they make of what they've read—not what *I've* told them, but what *they* think. Now I offer much shorter introductions to work. There are a lot of great videos available online, with tangential information, to get them started thinking in the ways the essays want them to, and I still use these. I think they are a little more interested in reading "Self-Reliance" when they see a video in which Robert Greene says he loved Emerson's essay so much he memorized the whole thing. Or another by a guy (Brian Johnson from *PhilosophersNotes*) who is such a big fan he named his son Emerson. I require them to read the essay. But these videos show them that they might *like* it. So instead of setting out groaning at the prospect of reading Emerson's twenty pages, they will think, "Hmm, okay, maybe this will be worth my time."

Another piece of advice Sun Tzu gives related to luring the opposition to the battlefield is "If they have advantage, entice them." This means use their "advantage" or energy against them. In other words, when they think they have the upper hand, let them use it. Why? Because a samurai doesn't win battles by only moving forward. Sometimes the samurai lets the opponent advance, knowing it will create an opportunity for an even stronger counterattack. For example, there are lots of things your students may know more about than you do—trends, technology, memes, slang, social media, et cetera. One way to take advantage of their advantage is to have them write about what they think they know about—encouraging them to show off a bit. Not only will this lead to some interesting topics (and you are a curious person, always ready to learn, right?), students will reveal themselves, which decreases their advantage. And once they've put what they know on paper, they've entered your territory, where most of the advantages will be yours. Don't be afraid to give assignments on topics you know little or nothing about (so long as it is relevant to what you have planned for the semester).

For example, traditional undergrads can write about what it's like to be a young adult in contemporary society. Adult students can write about their jobs or families. They can all write about their hobbies or interests or career goals. In some ways, you'll be the ideal reader, completely ignorant, needing background information, explanations, et cetera. But if you let them start by writing about something they know, at some point in the process, you'll be able to show them that they don't know as much as they thought they did, or that they are failing to clearly explain what they do know. If they don't recognize this themselves, you need to show them that there are problems they can't ignore. The solution to the problem: more thinking, more reading, and more writing. And they'll *want* to do it because they won't want to give up their advantage. But they will be doing the work you want them to, and you have regained control.

Once you are directing your students' energies, you need to be sure you are pointing them down the right paths because, as Sun Tzu says, "One who does not know the mountains and forests, gorges and defiles, swamps and wetlands, cannot advance the army." This means you can't let your students follow dead-end paths, get stuck in the muck that young writers are drawn to. I have found that

even after I have directed them to good topics for responses and shorter papers, too many of them still want to write
their research papers on tired, worn-out (boring) topics
like the death penalty, if college athletes should get paid, or
the genetic modification of foods. "No, no, no," I say. Their
research topic is the one they will spend the most time on
during the semester—thinking about it, reading about it,
and writing about it, which means it is the most important
one, through which they can learn the most. So only let
them choose topics that require critical thinking and will
lead to discovery. Only let them choose a research question they don't know the answer to and genuinely want to.

Also make sure that writing the research paper is a
long, multi-stage process for them—beginning with a
research proposal, including at least one individual conference, presented in multiple drafts, et cetera. If you allow
them to just turn something in, that's what they'll do. And
no matter how sound your plan is, some students will veer
off course, or onto some of these overly familiar paths.
When this happens, redirect them, for example, "No, I
don't think a paper on the use of steroids in baseball will
allow you to meet all the goals of the assignment. Maybe
a paper on *why* people cheat at sports would be more
interesting." Present ideas in a way that lets students make
the decisions; just be sure you cut off their inclinations to
get on the wrong path, be clear about why the path you are
pointing them towards is better in the end, and, in the end,
they'll be glad you did.

However you proceed (and I know enough to know I
don't know all the ways to proceed), remember that luring

students to the battlefield (as opposed to forcing them
onto it or expecting they'll show up on their own) gives
you an advantage, puts you in a position of control, and
greatly increases your ability to do the kind of teaching
you need to do.

Being Spontaneous

Sun Tzu says, "Your strategy for victories in battle is not repetitious, and your formations in response to the enemy are endless." In the classroom, while planning is important, it's not the only thing. You can't operate by rote. This is because every class, every student, is different. Just like they say about rivers, you can't step in the same classroom twice. Each student in every class has a unique genetic makeup, a lifetime of experiences, thoughts about writing and life, et cetera, so, of course, involving them in the progression of the class means it will be shaped in unexpected ways. This doesn't mean you simply walk into the classroom and see what happens—there need to be clear learning objectives for the students each day and strategies to reach them. It's the getting there that requires you to be adaptable.

Sun Tzu also says, "An army does not have constant force, or have constant formation." This means you shouldn't be rigid, don't try to "march" through the semester, don't try to "train" your students like dogs—repetition, repetition, repetition, then reward or punishment. Set your goals, but plan only the first engagement. Wait to see what happens before embarking on the next, and then

the next, and then again. To make this work, you need to
be observant, adaptable, and open. I don't want to say it's
got to be like jazz, because that would be a cliché, but you
get my drift . . . you may walk into the classroom planning one lesson, and then a student asks a question and
takes things in a different direction, one that introduces
new ideas about the topic, theme, structure, whatever. If
this seems promising, go there. You can always go back to
your planned lesson, and you must, but don't be afraid of
the unexpected. Maybe one day as class begins, the skies
darken, rain falls, and you have them write about that for
a bit. Another day, you may have a cold and don't want to
talk that much—so instead of forging ahead and risking
a coughing fit, ask them all to write a short essay about
being sick, the joys of being sick. Break them into groups
to brainstorm for ten minutes about why being sick is really better than being at full health, what one can learn
from illness. Whatever the day brings, be open-minded to
different ways a person can see the world.

Sun Tzu says, "Use the common to engage the enemy
and the uncommon to gain victory." The common, or
direct attack, is what they expect from the class: sitting
in desks, listening to you talk, watching you write words
on the board, reading some stuff, writing some stuff,
homework assignments, due dates, getting grades at the
end of the semester. The common attack is also the regular
discussion about writing a paper: introductions, thesis
statements, topic sentences, paraphrasing, summarizing,
quoting from a source, responding to these quotes, conclusions. These are all key parts of a composition course.

But you can't just attack Bad Writing this way because it's also important to keep your students on their toes, to design the class with "the uncommon" to keep it lively and interesting. The uncommon refers to your surprise attacks, the times you'll be coming at them in unexpected ways. As I said, you must be spontaneous, unorthodox, and full of surprises. Being spontaneous is important, but, by definition, hard to plan for. However, it is easy to plan activities students don't expect, which will have some of the same positive effects as spontaneously generated activities—reaching them from different angles, helping them feel they are *experiencing* something as opposed to "being taught."

This is important because, as Sun Tzu says, you should "attack where they are not prepared, go out to where they do not expect." What kind of surprise attacks do I suggest? As I've already mentioned, writing in unfamiliar forms is great—freewriting, dialogue, forms of poetry. A small-group exercise writing a Shakespearean sonnet on the value of revision is golden. Of course, that takes some time. Writing haiku is more efficient and is always a good use of time as it forces them to think—about ideas, language, precision, no matter what the topic. This is because:

> Writing a haiku
> means opening the mind and
> finding the right words

And that's essentially what writing is, right? I often assign assignments with a specific number of words required, like a 101-word summary of or response to an article we've read. This way I know that editing and revision, thinking about words, will be key parts of the process.

A writing-themed scavenger hunt is one of my favorite ways to surprise them. One day, usually almost halfway through the semester, after some real work has been done, after some grades have been given, as they settle in for another day in the classroom, I'll pass out a sheet of paper with a series of questions and challenges that requires them to get up and go on an adventure around campus. I ask them to describe people, places, things, impressions. I ask them to find my office and draw a map showing how to get there. I'll throw in some questions related to the course readings or their papers. I send them to the library, cafeteria, art gallery, or outdoors. But wherever they go, they must have an objective and write something. They see it as a series of tasks or challenges; I see it as a way to get them to appreciate writing as a way to better understand the world and themselves. Another benefit for me is the sublime peacefulness of sitting in the empty classroom with all my students' backpacks and jackets and books keeping me company—knowing they're out there writing haiku, eavesdropping on strangers, or doing their best to find the words that capture the smells of the library. I used to get a little anxious when I first started this exercise, thinking they should be doing something more serious. But when my students would return at the end of the class time, with a page full of freshly written words and smiles on their faces, I knew the time had been well spent, and that it would make the long days in the classroom seem more purposeful.

You should also go off the syllabus sometimes and have them write about unexpected topics or read surprising things. Most semesters, I choose a day and pass out a selection of six or seven Emily Dickinson poems. A couple of my favorite shorter ones are:

I HAD a daily bliss
I half indifferent viewed,
Till sudden I perceived it stir,—
It grew as I pursued,

Till when, around a crag,
It wasted from my sight,
Enlarged beyond my utmost scope,
I learned its sweetness right.

For each ecstatic instant
We must in anguish pay
In keen and quivering ratio
To the ecstasy

For each beloved hour
Sharp pittances of years
Bitter contested farthings
And coffers heaped with tears

On these days, I'll break the class into groups and give them ten to fifteen minutes to analyze one of the poems. And by analyze, I mean wrap their heads around what the poem *says*, what the poem *means*, how they can relate it to their own lives. This is always time well spent as it clears their minds and makes them think. Then I have them read the poems and share their responses with the rest of the class. It's wonderful.

Sometimes if I read something interesting and relevant while I'm drinking my morning coffee, I'll make copies of it. This may just be something to read together at the beginning or end of class, sometimes I'll have them do more with it. I've already mentioned the article I found saying there was proof that the current generation of college students was the most narcissistic in history. Another good one was the study that said Facebook makes people lonely, and the one that argued most college students are literally (physically) addicted to their cell phones. Maybe you will find an op-ed piece or comic strip or article from *The Onion* that is appropriate—make copies of that. The world is full of material. Use it.

While you always want to be productive, you don't always need to have a specific lesson in mind when you go off the syllabus—part of being a writer is just paying attention to things, being interested in things. Always keep that big picture in mind. They don't need to break down everything they read like the works they incorporate into formal assignments. The class, the readings, the assignments, the exercises are all just tools. The key is to develop curiosity, open-mindedness, and appreciation for language in your students, no matter what the topic is.

Some teachers are so dynamic, they can keep their students enraptured from the start of class to the end just with their good looks and the melodious power of their voices. I'm not one of them. And while I know it's wrong to make assumptions, I'm assuming you are not one of these teachers either. To keep your brood from falling into a lull, mix up your classroom strategies—watch video clips (Google relevant topics for half an hour and you'll find plenty of good stuff—funny takes on grammar, Weird Al Yankovic videos, comedy bits about palindromes), break into groups to solve writing-related problems of one sort or another. Of course, the core of the class and the bulk of the work needs to be writing, reading, thinking about writing, revision, practice, and more writing, but don't get stuck in a rut doing the same old thing every day or that's what you'll get in return: the same blank faces from the first day of class, the same tired, old essays that have been turned in for years. Activating them to think about the world and about writing in different ways will lead to more interesting writing. Let's face it, you're going to spend a lot of time reading those papers, a lot of your mental energy thinking about them—do yourself a favor and help your students make them as interesting as they can.

Besides these unexpected activities, you can encourage spontaneity by keeping the semester schedule, and each day's lesson, somewhat open. Budget time into the schedule where you honestly don't know what will happen. This creates energy, for you and your students. A key to remember is that people learn and retain ideas and information best as a result of experiences, not when they are simply told things. Obviously, if you spent a whole semester just *telling* your students what good writing is, how to do it, and why it's important, they wouldn't learn nearly as much as if they'd spent the semester writing and having writing-related experiences. And I'm not breaking any ground when I say that people crave experiences, that experiences are what life is made up of.

Here's a relevant example. Not long ago, I went to a small-group training session. It was part of an every-other-week, yearlong hodgepodge of professional development sessions on leadership. There was a different presenter each week, so we never knew what to expect. But this night when the presenter began, he said *he* didn't know what to expect and was excited about what might happen over the course of the next two hours. As he was saying this, I could feel myself getting excited too. *Something* was going to happen, something unexpected, and something was going to be created right there in that room that night. I mean, isn't that the kind of place we all want to be?

Well, the presenter proceeded to open a PowerPoint presentation and spent the next two hours going through it slide by slide, explaining terms, discussing scenarios, rarely pausing to ask for questions, and all the questions he asked had right and wrong answers, so if no one in the group answered correctly, he would do it for us. Obviously, barring a power failure or medical emergency, he knew *exactly* what was going to happen for those two hours. As a result, despite my best efforts, I was not engaged. And as it was happening, I even felt a little resentment towards him. Not because of the presentation itself, but because he had promised us something else. I've been to meetings where the opening statement has been, "We have to cover a lot of ground in the next two hours, so just get comfortable and take in as much as you can," and I've gotten comfortable and paid attention, and made it through. Maybe the format he presented the information in was the best means available, but, you see, he promised an *experience* of some sort and didn't come through.

Of course, I'm not saying you should promise your students an experience. If you do this, your students may expect too much and you may feel pressured. Instead, I suggest you undersell the class, let them think they're just going to sit there and listen to you talk, or do the same old things they've done before, and then before they realize it, you're pulling your tricks out of the bag, you're asking them to do things, they're smack in the middle of an experience, time is flying, and everyone's engaged. And learning.

A simple test to know whether or not you are providing your students with experiences is if someone were to ask them what they did in composition class, they'd be able to answer the question in active voice with themselves as the subject: *I* analyzed an essay, *I* wrote an outline. *We* broke into groups and did peer review. It should never (or very rarely) be limited to: *My teacher . . .*

Now, the experiences may be short or long, directly related to writing or not, but to be an experience where one can learn, it must involve some kind of problem-solving. Obviously, those tied to writing and language are best for composition class, but anything that requires critical thinking is good because that's a big part of what writing is, right? Problem-solving. Critical thinking. The words are just the means to express the solution to the problem. Sometimes all you need to do is ask (and get answers to) provocative questions: "Does religious belief improve a person's morality? Do animals have a self? Does true love exist?" Just about any kind of question that leads to unexpected answers, and then more fresh territory, is a good one.

Emotional experiences count as experiences too. They are not problem-solving, but can still lead to discovery of emotions that can play a role in the students' work. For example, if you are reading Martin Luther King Jr's "Letter from Birmingham Jail," you could spend some class time watching videos of King speaking, or of peaceful protesters being jeered, hosed down, or attacked by police dogs. Not only will this help students contextualize the reading, it may get them more emotionally involved in the topic and make it more important for them than it otherwise would have been, help them to care. Because writers care about things, don't we? Isn't that what prompts us to write in the first place?

So, to sum up my thoughts on being spontaneous, remember it is important to keep your students on their toes at all times, and you need to be on yours too, because the battle between The Way (which leads to good writing, clear use of language, development of ideas, constant engagement, an appreciation of the process) and The Wrong Way (which includes not just Bad Writing, but everything that leads writers to produce it: bad habits, laziness, apathy, shortcuts, lessons learned from bad teachers, et cetera) will be constant. You need to not only believe in The Way, you need to embody The Way, always aware that The Wrong Way is conspiring against you, waiting for you to slip up. To stay in control, you must be always fully engaged, alert, like the samurai, who expects nothing, anticipates everything, and reacts without thinking. This is what I mean by being spontaneous.

Using Groups

Sun Tzu says, "Commanding of many is like commanding of a few. It is a matter of dividing them into groups." If you had only one student a semester, or just a few, you might think you could do a better job. In some ways, you could. But in other ways, a bigger class is better. There is more energy, more flavor. You know how food seems to taste better in a crowded, lively restaurant? It's kind of like that. And teaching a big class doesn't have to be proportionally harder. How to achieve this? I recommend using small groups in class regularly. Sometimes, you'll need to simply present information or have full-class discussions, but let's face it, it is easy for students to tune these out. Small groups tend to stay focused better than big ones, and they stay focused best when given specific tasks.

Before I get into examples, let me say that the key to making group work productive is making sure there are two different objectives: 1) the objective the students should achieve—what they should do, or produce, in the time they work in their groups; and 2) the objectives *you have* for your students. Often these will overlap, but they are not the same thing. For example, your students' objectives may be to read an opening paragraph of an essay and write a better thesis statement. Or maybe assess the effectiveness of the personal example used in a paper. Or generate strong topic sentences. Assess the strength of the summary of sources. Come up with three strategies for an introduction. These are their objectives, and you want them to learn something about this. But the objectives *you* have for your students go beyond that, because in addition to helping them learn about thesis statements, personal examples, topic sentences, presentation of sources, or introductions, you are teaching them how to read a draft, to appreciate the value of revision, and to see the value in working to help others.

Sometimes I'll give all groups the same set of tasks (or series of questions—always tied to the goals of the course, of course) and then lead a class discussion where they compare their responses. Some days we'll all read the same essay and then I'll have all the groups answer some simple questions: "What is the main point of this? What is the writer's objective? Who is the intended audience (and what leads you to believe that is the intended audience)?"

Before they write the first paper of the semester that asks them to summarize ideas from another writer and present quotes, I'll give them fifteen to twenty minutes in class to complete an exercise like this one:

- -

1. Present a direct quote from paragraph 1 of "Self-Reliance." Do this in three parts: introduce the quote (be sure to identify the author in a signal phrase),

present the quote (and page #), then respond to/
explain the quote.

2. Paraphrase (restate in your own words) the follow-
    ing passage from page 2 of "Self-Reliance": "There
    is a time in every man's education when he arrives at
    the conviction that envy is ignorance; that imitation
    is suicide; that he must take himself for better, for
    worse, as his portion; that though the wide universe
    is full of good, no kernel of nourishing corn can
    come to him but through his toil bestowed on that
    plot of ground which is given to him to till."

Other times, their tasks should be different, comple-
menting or opposing each other. For example, when I am
explaining rhetoric and rhetorical analysis to them, they
will all read the same essay, and then I'll have some groups
identify examples of the writer's use of ethos, other groups
identify pathos, and others identify logos. Another group
may try to discern the writer's biases. Then all the groups
will share what they have discovered. I have also found
groups seem to work better if they have to "present" the
highlights of their discussion with the rest of the class.

Whatever you ask them to do, it's important to always
give them something very specific *to do*, because if you
are too vague and ask them for nothing, nothing is exactly
what they'll give you. I have found it is best to ask them to
produce something—a written document they need to turn
in at the end of the class, something they need to put their

names on (this also makes it easy to take attendance and to assign the exercise to anyone who has missed class that day as out-of-class work). Besides the fact that having them write down their thoughts, ideas, responses, et cetera, is always a good idea, this helps compel them to act, and you can see if they are doing the work you need them to.

Still, it's not always that easy to make sure groups are working effectively, so I like to stroll around the room to check in on them, usually when they have been working for five minutes or so, asking questions, making sure they understand their objectives, that they can document their findings. Sometimes I "interrupt" sooner to tell students they need to sit closer to each other and face each other if they want to have a good discussion. Through trial and error, I can determine which students work well together and which to keep apart. The first time I break them into groups, I do it based on geography, that is, whoever is sitting close to each other. But as the semester goes on, I mix up the groups from time to time, make them move around the room so they don't get stuck in the same old discussions, with the same dynamics in play. Always make it fresh.

Group chemistry and dynamics are very important, of course, and you'll have to pay attention to this. Left on their own, some groups will just sit and stare at their desks or the handouts you've given them. Sometimes one person will do all the work, or they'll split into factions, or they'll talk about everything except what you have asked them to. As I said earlier, you'll need to mix and match the groups to avoid these problems. If a student is reserved, put him or her in a group with one who is not only confident but also conscientious enough to include everyone in the discussion, a natural leader. Sometimes it is good to put friends together. Other times it is better to split them up—if the dynamic between them or the roles they play with each other get in the way of them both being active participants. You usually don't want three loud, opinionated people in one group. However, I've had groups like this I've let stay together because no matter what the task, they would jump right in, all had good ideas to share, and engaged in interesting debates. They served as a model to the others, raised the volume in the room, and made it easier for the other groups to start to work and talk. It was also clear they were enjoying themselves, and no matter how I describe my job, getting in the way of anyone else's pleasure is not part of it.

The worst-case scenario when it comes to group work is total silence. I mean when all the groups are silent. Sometimes this is because the tasks given them are confusing or simply too difficult. Sometimes it takes them a while to get going, but if it's dead in the classroom, I go around to each group and ask if they have questions. If one group does, I'll repeat the question (and my answer) to the whole class, which can help get everyone going. Sometimes I need to clarify or revise the tasks I've asked of them. Or model the kind of thinking I need them to do before the groups engage in meaningful, productive work. Other times we will read something again, or something else, before I set them back to work.

One group exercise every composition class should utilize is peer review. Done properly, this is a great way to help students know the objectives of the course and assignments, develop skills for reading and revising, see that there are multiple points of view on both writing and whatever topics students are writing about, and achieve the mindset you want them to—to see themselves as good soldiers fighting to not only improve as writers but help their fellow soldiers improve their writing too. But this doesn't happen automatically. To utilize peer review most effectively, I suggest the following:

Before you begin the first time (and maybe every time you do peer review), explain the benefits of peer review. I tell my students there are many, including: 1) getting feedback on one's draft, 2) learning how to read more critically to see the strengths and weaknesses of a draft, 3) learning how to come up with solutions to problems on the draft, and 4) gaining a better understanding of the requirements for the assignment.

Here are the peer review guidelines I share with my class:

- Before you read the paper, read over the peer review sheet so you understand the questions you will be responding to.
- Before you make any comments, read the entire paper.
- If you are working in a group, discuss each question/subtopic on the peer review sheet before you write out your responses.

- When you respond, write in complete sentences so your feedback is clear to the writer.
- Keep in mind your goal is to share your responses (as a reader) to the paper and offer suggestions for revision, but it is not to "grade" or revise the paper.
- Remember to point out the strengths as well as the weaknesses of the document.
- Keep in mind that you are reviewing a rough draft and your classmate is engaged in the peer review process to gain insight into how well his or her current draft is/is not meeting the goals for the assignment.
- All your comments should be appropriate and constructive. Be respectful and considerate of the writer's feelings.
- Be sure that your comments are clear and focus on the text in the draft (for example, it is better to point to a specific sentence and say, "This sentence is unclear" as opposed to saying, "You are not being clear").
- Be as specific as possible with your responses so the writer will know what you are referring to. Responding with feedback such as "unclear" or "vague" is too general to be valuable. If something is not working, explain *why*. Likewise, if something in the paper does impress or captivate you, instead of just saying so, explain *why* it is working well.
- When possible, raise questions and/or suggest new, related subtopics that may not have occurred to the writer.

- Do not attempt to revise any grammatical or stylistic errors. You can point out issues and/or unclear sentences, but do not "rewrite" the paper (that is the writer's responsibility).
- While you should give valuable feedback/constructive criticism, do not overwhelm the writer with too much. Focus mainly on filling out the peer review form and answering the questions raised there.
- Be aware of your opinions and/or biases and do not let them affect the feedback you give your classmates. While you may not agree with the writer's argument or stance on the issue being discussed, you can still provide valuable responses about how well the paper is meeting the assignment objectives.
- Keep in mind that while the objective of a peer review session is to provide feedback to a fellow writer, an important benefit of taking this process seriously is that it will help you as a writer—first, as a way to better understand the objectives of the current assignment, and secondly, as a way to help you develop the skills you need to revise your own writing in the future.
- When in doubt at any time throughout this process, remember to follow the Golden Rule of Peer Review: treat your classmates' papers as you want yours to be treated and give the type of feedback you would like to receive.
- As always, if you have questions, ask your instructor for clarification.

- -

The process I have found works best for peer review goes like this: students come to class with four copies of their rough draft (obviously, work has been done before this—discussing the assignment, writing responses, doing exercises, developing thesis statements, et cetera). I tell them to bring copies of the papers without their names, but as I'm collecting them, I have them write their names on one copy so I know whose is whose. I arrange all the drafts on a spare desk, then go over the peer review sheet in detail, reading and explaining the questions and directing them how to answer them. I break the students into groups (three is the ideal number) then distribute the drafts to the groups. As you will see, my suggestions for and description of peer review are for in-person classes, so if you are teaching virtually, my advice is to try to replicate this as closely as possible and use groups if you can (as opposed to individual reviews) as the discussions on the drafts are valuable for the students and the feedback produced from groups tends to be better than feedback from individuals.

Before I show you the peer review sheet I use for my students' papers on "Self-Reliance," I'm going to show you the assignment sheet. Then you can see how this clearly corresponds to and previews the questions on the peer review sheet.

Analysis of "Self-Reliance"

For this paper, you need to present Emerson's main points in "Self-Reliance" and then use a specific idea from the essay as a "critical lens" to write an analysis/argument about a contemporary issue/topic.

Your key objectives for the 3 parts of the paper are to:
1. Sum up Emerson's main argument in "Self-Reliance"
2. Discuss one specific idea from "Self-Reliance"
3. Present an argument about a contemporary topic—related to the specific idea from Part 2

In Part 1 of your paper (2+ pages), your goal is to accurately sum up Emerson's argument, writing as if your reader has not read "Self-Reliance." To provide a good summary, answer some or all of the following questions (though you do not need to limit yourself to these):

- How does Emerson define self-reliance?
- According to Emerson, why is it difficult to be self-reliant?
- What are the benefits of being self-reliant?
- What are the negative consequences of *not* being self-reliant?

Be sure to include evidence from the text to support your points. Present 4-5 direct quotations and present them like this: Emerson says, "Envy is ignorance" (2).

In Part 2, you need to present a specific idea (with a quote). For example, you could present Emerson's idea that "Travelling is a fool's paradise" (17) or the idea "we are ashamed of that divine idea which each of us represents" (2) or his claim that "man postpones or remembers; he does not live in the past, but with reverted eye laments the past, or, heedless of the riches that surround him, stands on tiptoe to foresee the future" (11) and use that as a jumping off point to make your argument (Part 3) about something happening in the world today.

For Part 3, you need to present your own argument about self-reliance, somehow related to the idea you have presented in Part 2 of the paper. Contemporary topics may focus on social, political, or religious issues; personal experiences; philosophical questions; et cetera. Your argument may be a combination of agreeing and disagreeing with Emerson. For this part of the paper, you need to go beyond simply stating your opinion and **support your position.** The best way to do this is to provide **specific examples** that support your position (examples from your own life or things you've observed).

A successful paper will go into great detail, both explaining Emerson's ideas, and the contemporary issue, and making valid, interesting points connecting these topics.

As you begin to work on this project, don't think of it as a matter of writing down what you already know—think of the writing process as a way to gain a better understanding of the topic you choose.

You can use anything you have written in your earlier response to "Self-Reliance" in this paper, but be aware that your understanding of his argument has likely changed since you wrote that.

<u>Aim for 5-6 pages. An outline might look like this:</u>
- Introduction with a well-developed thesis statement (1/2 page)
- General summary of "Self-Reliance," with quotes (2 pages)
- Discussion of the specific idea from "Self-Reliance," with quotes (1/2 page)
- Analysis/argument on the contemporary issue you've chosen, with specific examples (2 pages)
- Conclusion (1/2 page)

- -

Now I will show you the questions on the peer review sheet. Because I also use this for grading the papers, I try to make it perfectly clear to them what the assignment objectives are and how they will be graded. After each question, I leave enough space for the students to write at least two or three well-developed sentences so it takes up at least both sides of a sheet of paper.

- -

Analysis of "Self-Reliance" Peer Review

1. How well does the introduction introduce the topic and engage the reader?

2. Does the thesis statement identify Emerson and 1) state his main argument in "Self-Reliance," 2) state the specific subtopic from the essay the writer is focusing on, and 3) present the writer's argument about a contemporary topic? (Remember, the thesis statement should not leave the reader asking any How? or Why? questions.)

3. Part 1 of the paper: How well does the paper present Emerson's argument? Would a reader who has not read "Self-Reliance" understand Emerson's main points? Does the paper include relevant quotes that help make Emerson's argument clear to the reader? Are the quotes introduced properly? Does the writer explain the quotes for the reader's benefit?

4. Part 2 of the paper: After summing up Emerson's argument, does the paper focus on a specific idea from Emerson's essay (with at least one quote)?

5. Part 3 of the paper: Does the paper present a compelling argument based on a specific idea from Emerson? Does it present reasons and support (specific examples) for these reasons? Is the argument a good one? Is it interesting? Does it go beyond the obvious? Why or why not?

6. Does this paper have a conclusion that sums up the main points, restates the thesis statement, and leaves a lasting impression?

7. Is this paper well organized? Does each paragraph focus on a subtopic? Does each subtopic relate to the thesis? Do paragraphs begin with topic sentences? Are transitions between paragraphs (and ideas) smooth?

8. Rate the paper's grammar, clarity, and readability: Needs improvement (lots of mistakes and confusing sentences), Developing (readable, but needs substantial improvements), Proficient (only minor revisions needed), Advanced (a pleasure to read and I couldn't find any errors).

9. Other comments and at least 3 suggestions for revision.

10. Suggest a good title for this paper (it may refer to "Self-Reliance," but remember that argument only makes up half of the paper).

- -

Some of these are Yes/No questions, which I found could be problematic in that they could be answered in a single word, so now I require students to explain their answers with two or three complete sentences that refer specifically to the content of the paper being reviewed. I tell my students I should know what the paper focuses on just by reading the peer review sheet and they are not allowed to repeat any of the language from the questions in their answers. I learned this the hard way, with too many students responding with comments like:

This paper is well organized, each paragraph focuses on a subtopic, and each subtopic relates to the thesis. Paragraphs begin with topic sentences, and transitions between paragraphs (and ideas) are smooth.

Even if this is true, without explaining *why* it is true, this is not helpful to either the writer or the reviewers.

For peer review, I don't put students in groups with their own drafts. There are two reasons for this—first, while there is a benefit to being privy to the group's critiques, I don't think composition students are ready for this. For the writer (remember, many of them are anxious about their writing, and themselves), the twenty to twenty-five minutes listening to classmates read their draft and discuss its merits will probably be the worst, most uncomfortable, anxiety-producing minutes of the day, if not the entire semester. Equally important, the other group members will not engage in the kind of frank, in-depth critiques they need to if the writer is sitting right beside them. Ideally, students' drafts are on the other side of the room because I know when some students hear their classmates discussing their paper, they will get distracted from the paper in front of them, the one they should be giving feedback on.

Once all groups have their drafts, I tell them to read them to themselves (some teachers like it if all groups read aloud, but I've found the noise of others reading is more distracting than actual conversations), then when everyone in the group has finished reading, to begin to discuss and answer the questions on the peer review sheet. I tell them they should comment on the drafts and that they can mark grammatical errors and confusing passages, but warn against going crazy copy-editing, as this is not their job (and I've had some students start to do this and be barely a page into a draft when the rest of the group is already done reading and ready to begin discussion).

I will also have a copy of every draft being reviewed and typically have time to read over the first page and maybe flip through the rest while the groups are working. As groups are working, I go around and ask if they have questions, answering them if I can and repeating to the class as needed. When a group is finished, or think they are, I go to them and look over the peer review sheet to make sure they have answered all questions clearly, in sufficient detail, and in complete sentences. If they have responded incorrectly or not gone far enough explaining their responses, or have been too nice or too critical, I direct them how to make changes. The feedback they give will not be perfect, but I want to be sure that when the writer gets the peer review sheet back at the end of the week, there is some usable, valuable feedback.

Once the peer review sheet has been filled out to my satisfaction, I collect it along with the papers (which they are also required to write feedback on) and then give the group another set of drafts and a clean peer review sheet. I never give any of the drafts or completed peer review sheets back to the students until all papers have been reviewed. Because peer review typically lasts more than one day, this means I have to carry an extra thick stack of papers to and from class on those days and I have to keep them organized: completed, started but not completed, not started yet. It's a bit of a hassle but a small price to pay to make sure all students come back for the second day of peer review (which was not always the case when a student's paper had been returned after day one).

That is the process that works for me. Now on to the benefits. The one the students may be most interested in the first time they do peer review is the practical one of getting feedback on their writing. Their classmates have the task of identifying the strengths and weaknesses of the draft. They give suggestions the writer can use as a guide for revision before turning a paper in for a grade. This is undeniably valuable. However, the first time a class does peer review, a lot of students don't give (or consequently get) great feedback. This is because they're just starting to wrap their heads around the process, may not yet know exactly how to achieve the goals of the assignment, and may focus too much on some tired, old rules left over from their previous English classes. So, in a way, I use the first round of peer review to help teach them how to do peer review. They'll do better the second time through, and better than that the third. So the first experience with peer review is kind of like a rough draft, full of mistakes, but it is time well spent because that's how they learn.

The biggest benefit of peer review is the development of the skills needed to read a draft: to see the strengths and weaknesses, how well it is meeting the objectives of the assignment, and then be able to give clear, practical advice on how to revise the paper. But make sure your students go far enough. Don't let them just identify problems—make them explain *why* a flaw is a flaw and propose a solution. If the writer's tone is not appropriate, I'll ask them to point to specific words or phrases that show this. If an example or comparison doesn't work, I have them explain why and suggest a better one. I tell my students that being in a composition class, one that focuses on the process, includes class time for peer review, and allows revisions on all graded papers, is a gift. I tell them for just about every paper they will write for other classes, the teacher will give them an assignment and a due date and maybe point them in a direction before saying, "See you on the other side."

I tell them what they are learning in composition class is how to make best use of that time between getting the assignment and the due date. The steps of the process incorporated into a writing class are the very ones they need to incorporate into their own writing process. I tell them that the ability to step back from one's own draft, to read it as a reader, not as the writer, is one that can best be learned by going through a number of peer review sessions. Learning how to turn off the creative, generative (and oftentimes sloppy) mind and turning on the clear, critical thinking mind is invaluable for a writer. I tell this to them over and over, and hopefully over the course of the semester, they begin to believe that what I say is true.

The final benefit of peer review is that students, no matter what else happens, should come out of it with a clear understanding of the objectives for the assignment. Many students need to be told more than once what the objectives for the assignment are. I'm always amazed how far off some students are when they turn in initial drafts, even when I have spelled out clearly on the assignment sheet what is required, even after I've spent class time talking about it, writing instructions on the board, showing them samples of what to and what not to do, even having them write outlines in class. "Yes, that looks good," I'll say when I read the outline. "Write your paper based on that!" And then they'll come to class with a rough draft that goes in a completely different direction. But after engaging in peer review, measuring drafts against the assignment objectives multiple times, it should be clear what their paper is *supposed* to be doing.

Before I move on, there are a few more keys to making sure this time is spent effectively. First, it is important to model the kind of critique you want them to engage in. Before the first peer review session, we do a sort of sample peer review, either with a response paper students have recently submitted or a completed paper from a previous semester. Everyone gets the same paper, we read it aloud one paragraph at a time, I write a series of questions on the board, similar to what they'll see on the peer review sheet, then they'll break into groups for ten or fifteen minutes discussing these, then we'll discuss it as a class. If it is a response paper, I collect these one day, choose one or two to make copies of, and distribute them (without the writers' names) to the class the next day. I tell them I select them randomly, but I always choose samples that will make for interesting discussions, ones that will allow me (or better yet, a student) to make an important point about either the subject written about or the way it has been written.

For this exercise, it's important to remember that students can learn just as much looking at a bad draft as good ones. But it's also important to know that students can be ruthless when they are "critiquing" an anonymous draft, and if the first person to speak has a negative comment, that can gain momentum quickly, everyone piling on, and the writer can feel attacked and crushed. To make sure that does not happen, focus the discussion on strengths and weaknesses, always on the paper and not the writer. Model and get them to appreciate the right kind of reading and responding needed for the effective peer review sessions they'll be engaged in later in the semester. That is not to say you want everyone to be nice, but if a student comes up to you in tears at the end of the class after his or her work has been discussed (yes, this has happened to me), you have probably let things go too far in the wrong direction. To avoid this, what I do now whenever possible is use samples from another section, either another one I am teaching that semester, or some I've held on to from previous semesters (assuming the assignment is the same). This way, I can be sure students won't be anxious, and when I tell the class that the writer of the piece they are responding to is not in the classroom, all students feel more freedom to respond with more candor. If you must use samples from the class you are teaching, I advise you use papers that are generally strong (but still with a few weaknesses you can discuss).

Another key to making sure peer review works is to nurture a positive, helpful attitude amongst the troops. Hopefully, you've been exhibiting this all along, in your own special way, and your students should naturally follow suit, but always remind them as you begin a day of peer review to follow the Golden Rule of Peer Review, which means give the sort of feedback they would like to get in return. This means, among other things: be fair, be honest, give constructive criticism (and praise), provide solutions to problems, and write the feedback with the knowledge that the writer has not been a part of their conversation. Sometimes groups are too nice (or sometimes just lazy) and write things like, "Everything looks great!" These groups typically need to be told to look at the draft with a more critical eye.

If a group says something looks good, even after I raise my doubts, I'll ask them to explain *why*, first aloud to me, and then on the peer review sheet (of course, this often leads to a re-analysis and revision of their comment). Other groups have the opposite problem and are too critical, finding fault with everything, mistakenly thinking that is the objective of the exercise. This is probably the result of some bad writing teachers in the past. I tell these groups to be a little gentler, to point out weaknesses and strengths, to give the writer suggestions for improvement.

Another important part of the process is that after all the drafts have been reviewed, before you hand them back to the students, assuming you've been paying attention to the drafts and the feedback and jotting down notes to yourself along the way, take some time to go over what you have noticed: citation errors, a misunderstanding of assignment objectives, grammar problems, whatever you think is important for them to think about before they start to revise.

Sometimes I will write passages from drafts, good or bad, on the board for quick discussions. After I hand back their drafts, I usually give them all a revision or writing-related task to complete before they leave for the day or for the next day. Some examples of these are:

What was the most valuable feedback you received from your classmates?

What is the one change you plan to make when you revise this paper to submit for grading?

What did you see, either good or bad, in a class-mate's paper that has helped you better understand how to revise your own paper?

Even if I don't ask them to do anything, I like to hand back the drafts and peer review sheets with five to ten minutes left in class. I ask them to look things over and ask questions before they leave for the day. I remind them that it is an imperfect process and that the feedback they are getting is just that: feedback. It doesn't mean they have to do everything suggested. But I tell them that reading over the feedback carefully is an important part of their revision process, and, as always, to let me know if they have any questions.

If I think it will help, I will even type up a "Tips for Revision" sheet, like this one, and give it to the class:

Tips for revising your Analysis of "Self-Reliance"

- Open your paper with an introduction about your argument/analysis, then introduce/connect to Emerson and "Self-Reliance." Posing a question, giving a description, or sharing a brief anecdote/story related to your topic are all good strategies. The end of the opening paragraph will be your 3-part thesis statement:

  For your analysis of "Self-Reliance" your objectives are to:

  (1) Sum up Emerson's main argument in "Self-Reliance"
  (2) Discuss one specific idea from "Self-Reliance"
  (3) Present an argument about a contemporary topic—related to the specific idea from objective #2

  So, your thesis statement should have 3 parts and look something like this:

  (1) In "Self Reliance," Emerson argues that relying on one's self and resisting the conformist influences of society is the best way to achieve one's potential. (2) One point he brings up is that people should never rely on others. (3) I disagree with this point

because I believe following good role models is a way to develop one's self and grow.

(1) In "Self Reliance," Emerson argues that relying on one's self and resisting the conformist influences of society is the best way to achieve one's potential. (2) One point he brings up is that travel should be avoided because it can lead one away from his or her true self. (3) I disagree with this point because I think travel, or getting out of one's comfort zone in another way, encourages one to better understand one's self and develop self-reliance.

(1) In "Self Reliance," Emerson argues that relying on one's self and resisting the conformist influences of society is the best way to achieve one's potential. (2) One point he brings up is that desiring what others have leads one away from his or her true potential. (3) I agree with this point because I have seen many people focus their energy on being like celebrities or social media influencers and, as a result, lose track of their God-given uniqueness.

- Include Emerson's full name (Ralph Waldo Emerson) and the title of his essay ("Self-Reliance") in the introduction (after that, refer to him by last name only).
- Do not put quotes from Emerson in the introduction or thesis statement. If a quote is worth including, it should be in the body of the paper and clearly explained (which you shouldn't do in the introduction).

- Be objective/impartial for Part 1 of the paper (your goal here is to present and explain Emerson's ideas, not agree/disagree with them or make references to society today). For this part of the paper, you <u>must write in third-person point of view</u> (do not use: *you, your, I, we,* or *us*).

- For Part 2 of the paper, you need to SHOW your reader that what you say is true. The best way to do this is with actual, specific examples (not hypothetical examples, which don't "prove" anything). For example, instead of saying, "People try to act like influencers they see on social media," say, "A girl I knew in high school wanted so much to be like Kendall Jenner she got her hair cut just like her, started copying her wardrobe, started talking like her, and only liked things she said she liked, like blueberry yogurt (even though she was allergic to blueberries and ended up in the hospital)." For this part of the paper, you can write in third-person point of view and first-person point of view (I…). There should not be any new quotes from Emerson in this section, but you can refer to quotes and ideas you have presented earlier.

- If you are using any outside sources besides "Self-Reliance" (this is not required), include the title of the source and the author's full name in the body of the paper and include a Works Cited page. (If you are not using any other sources, you do not need a Works Cited page for this paper.)

- -

I've heard some teachers say that putting students in groups is taking the easy way out. They say this as criticism, but in some ways I agree—because it can be an *easy* way to unite the class, make you more efficient, and put your students in a better position to learn and meet their goals. Remember that just because something is harder for you does not mean it is better for your students. One of the things I like about peer review is that my students are working hard (and learning) and I'm not. I can kind of coast through these days, storing up my energy for grading the next round of drafts. Other teachers resist peer review because they think it ends up being "amateur hour" that produces no good feedback. If that's the case, it's the teacher's fault. The teacher needs to teach the students how to give feedback. If peer review is done properly, everyone can benefit.

Getting Students Invested In Their Writing

Part of Sun Tzu's ability to get his soldiers to pay attention to him was the fact that they were being prepared for battle, life-or-death situations. Being proficient, skillful, knowledgeable, and aware meant survival, while any of the opposites meant death. Suffice to say, it paid to pay attention and do the work in training. To the extent that you can, you need to instill the same attitudes in your students, as if saying to them: If your life was in jeopardy and you had one chance to explain yourself, to save yourself with something you've written, don't you want to be able to make that as clear and compelling as possible? Most of your students will not find themselves in situations where they need to write themselves to safety, but they will need to write well for class, to find jobs, to advance. They'll need to write love letters, apologies, and explanations. They'll need to write to understand what they think and how they feel. Lots of things in their lives will be dependent on how well they can write. They may not appreciate this at the start of the semester, and some won't at the end of it either, but you have got to open their minds to it, that Writing is The Way. That it matters. This is the key to getting them invested. Here are ten more ways to keep them engaged.

1. Make them think for themselves

Another good piece of motivational advice Sun Tzu gives is "If they are humble, make them haughty." But why haughty? Isn't humility better? In life, yes, but some students are too humble, to the point of, what's the word I'm looking for . . . timorous. Part of your job is to get them to think for themselves. They probably have not had to do this in their five-paragraph essays in high school. So if you ask them a question and they respond in a way that implies, "I don't know, you're the teacher, tell me what I should do," you need to reverse their thinking. Not to the point of the teacher whose students complained about the lack of direction and guidance they were given, but to the point where the students take it upon themselves to do the real work of the class.

Sometimes you'll come across students who, for one reason or another, don't seem to have the ability to think for themselves. My guess is that they have been told or taught that all knowledge must come from an outside sources, from authorities. Students like these are almost the complete opposite of you, composition instructor (independent, free-thinking, creative), and they present you with one of your biggest challenges. Now these students won't cause trouble for you, but they'll resist growth, and you don't want your students to be the same at the end of the semester as in the beginning. For a student like this, the most typical answer, whatever the question, is "I don't know." Now it is true that sometimes the best possible answer to a question is "I don't know." Other times, that is a good *first* answer to a question. Because admitting you don't know the answer to a question opens it up to unlimited answers, unlimited possibilities. But you can't let it stop there. If "I don't know" is a valid terminal answer, you've asked the wrong kind of question. But if you have asked the right kind of question and your student still humbly says, "I don't know," you need to tell that student that even though the topic may be unfamiliar, it's possible to come up with an answer. Tell this student that each and every person on earth is living a life like no one else, because each has a unique biology, chemistry, and set of experiences that allows one to see the world through eyes unlike anyone else's. You can tell them they're all snowflakes if you have to—all special in their own way. But whatever it takes, they've all got to come up with *something*.

Hopefully, your conversations will be more productive than the one I once had with one of my students in a developmental writing class. She was trying to come up with a topic, any topic, on which to base a simple argument. It had to be at least mildly controversial, as in there had to be at least two sides and each side had to have reasons. I was not necessarily asking her to write about this topic, I just wanted her to understand what an argument was. I began with a simple question on the topic of the ethics of eating meat.

"Should people eat meat?" I asked her.

"I don't know."

"Do you eat meat?"

"Yes."

"Why do you eat meat?"

"I don't know."

"Do you like how it tastes?"

"Yes."

"Why?"

"I don't know."

"But you do know that you like the taste, right?"

"Yes."

"Okay, so you're saying one reason we should eat meat is because it's delicious. See, you do know about this. Now what's another reason we should eat meat?"

"I don't know . . ."

Now this student was particularly "humble," and I had to spell out a few reasons both for and against eating meat and hope she could formulate an argument based on that, but typically once you get them started, they can generate ideas on their own. If the ideas students come up with are too simple, or too familiar, encourage them to look deeper into the question, look at it from a different angle.

For example, if a student wants to argue that the media's presentation of an idealized, unrealistic female body image leads to eating disorders, why do only a small percentage of teenage girls develop eating disorders? What other factors contribute to this? Or maybe get that student to think about the fact that young boys' minds are also warped by society's presentation of female beauty—they can only value a girl based on what she is *supposed* to

look like. One way or another, get them to say something
unique, reach out to try new things. This generates a lot
of energy for students and gets them thinking in the right
ways. I encourage my students to go too far in their thinking as opposed to not far enough. They will make mistakes,
but they need to know that's a necessary part of the game.
Because if they just play it safe, they won't make the sort of
discoveries you need them to, the ones that will keep them
interested.

2. Don't let them coast

Another of Sun Tzu's rules is "If they are relaxed, toil
them." As you surely have been disheartened to discover,
sometimes students can be very lazy, both in the classroom and in their work. These students are easy to spot
but difficult to change. You need to get them invested, to
see that the class is not just about the grade, but that their
very lives are at stake. If they don't care about their lives,
well, that's an even bigger challenge for you. Surprisingly,
some of your stronger students may be lazy too—those
with some talent and experience with writing may want
to slide through the whole semester doing passable work
without investing much effort. But this won't lead to
growth. Some students *will* be invested more easily because they want to do well in the class or because of a
genuine interest in learning (Yes, there are students like
that in composition class. I mean, weren't you like that?
If not, don't you wish you would've been?). But whatever

the makeup of each class is, they all need to get invested in the work of the class.

Sometimes students will bring energy in the beginning of the semester, make strides early, then ease into a comfortable groove with plans to coast the rest of the way. You need to find new ways to challenge this type of student too. Luckily, with writing, there is never an end to it—everyone can always get better. Just keep in mind that the kind of "toil" you are aiming for is productive, invigorating, active, the kind that not only produces growth, but enthusiasm. If I sense a student is having too easy a time writing an argument, whether it be in favor of hunting, homeschooling, or hedonism, I'll ask for three pages from the opposing point of view, written so well that they are forced to question their original stance. Sometimes I have them write the same argument in a different voice. Not a whole new paper, but just a short, little exercise to keep them thinking. When I was coaching runners, sometimes I'd have them run backwards, or sideways, or in some other exaggerated way, with high knees, with faster footfalls. When they got back to their regular form, it felt different, better. It's the same with writing. Use variety to be always building momentum. The possibilities are endless, but the key is to keep them active, never coasting.

3. Acknowledge different learning styles

Another way to keep them active is to mix up your methods of delivery. Yes, you must know your strengths and weaknesses. Are you better at lecturing, PowerPoints, small groups, individual conferences? Find out and take advantage of the skills you have. At the same time, the class is not about what you can do well—it's about what your students learn to do well. (To take that further, though I've written a book telling you lots about what to do, the semester is not about what *you* do, it's about what your students do. Don't ever forget that.)

So you must acknowledge different learning styles. You might love whole-class discussions, but some of your students might not get a lot out of it. Start with small groups, or give them writing prompts before the discussion to be sure everyone has engaged with the ideas of the day. If you need to lecture, be sure to give your students visuals to clarify your points. This can be a simple PowerPoint, writing on the board, or handouts you work through together. It's the rare student that can sit and understand and appreciate what you simply say. You should assume that even those who are capable will start daydreaming after a few minutes. Most students need to *see* things to really have them stick. And for some people (myself included) writing something down is the best way to get it to stick in the brain. Let them know this. You can even spend half a class session reading about learning styles. Because it's a writing (and reading) class, you can explore any topic and never be off topic. Ask them which style they think works best for them. Try to use all of them. Follow up later in the semester to make sure you haven't fallen into a rut and ignored the needs of some students.

4. Keep asking questions

You'll also keep your students engaged if you create a natural critical learning environment—one where people are always asking questions. For example, after my students read an essay on memory and the self, and I want them to discuss the extent to which one's self depends on memory, I'll ask hypothetical questions like: If a person lost all memories and had to start anew, would that person have the same self, be the same person as before? Why or why not? To what extent? Sometimes to get started on this topic, we have spent big chunks of time talking about movies that focus on memory loss. There are lots of them (*The Bourne Identity, 50 First Dates, The Notebook, The Vow, Eternal Sunshine of the Spotless Mind, Total Recall, Overboard, Finding Nemo*, et cetera), and most college students love talking about movies. And all the while they think they're just talking about movies, without knowing it, they'll be engaged in critical thinking and moving towards finding meaning.

Many students will come into class able to state their opinions, but that's not enough. Some will be able to state opinions and explain them at length. But that's still not enough. They need to present arguments, which means including reasons, which means looking at both sides of a topic, which means exploring previously unconsidered options, and writing clearly about all of it. Asking them questions about things that matter to them leaves them no choice but to do all this. For example: If you believe in God, explain genocide. If you don't believe in God, explain religion. If you believe in reincarnation, explain population growth. You get the idea. Ask questions that require a lot of thought. Base questions on what you know about your students and what you want to know. What's the happiest moment you've had in your life? What made it so great? Would you change anything about it if you could? You can't ask questions like that at a dinner party or a family picnic. But you can ask your students just about anything. Take advantage of the opportunity.

5. Help them make connections

Besides making your job easier, keeping your students active and engaged is also important because they won't learn if they are simply *receiving* information—because knowledge is something one needs to construct on his or her own. Think about the most important things you've learned in life: how to ride a bike, study for a test, or French kiss. Even if someone told you how to do this, you really didn't *learn* anything until you did so on your own. It's also true that the things we learn are based on the things we already know. That's why I like to focus my composition classes on the self, because my students already *know* themselves, at least to the extent that can lead them to more knowledge. They know their likes and dislikes, what they've done in life, their goals, how they generally feel about certain things, and these are all good starting points. Whatever you focus on in your class, it's critical that your students can make connections between what they already know and what you're trying to teach them. This is how knowledge develops and should be applied to both the topics you ask them to read about and the writing and reading processes they need to succeed.

Having them make connections between readings and ideas is probably something you are already doing. Making connections between ideas from readings and their own experiences can also be rather easy, if the readings are appropriate. For example, in Csikszentmihalyi's "What is the Self?" he says the car has become the one object that people use to project their ideal self onto the world. To test this theory, I ask my students about their cars, or the cars they'd like to have in the future. Or is it not the car? I ask them. Has the car been replaced by something else? The cell phone? Does it matter to them what kind of phone they have? Why? Or is it clothing? Or the house they live in? Or is it now something virtual, not tangible, like a social media account? These always end up being interesting and fruitful discussions.

It's a little trickier to get them to compare their writing to something else. Sometimes when I am handing back revised, regraded papers, wishing I could have given out higher grades than I have, I tell my students that writing a paper, especially when one engages in multiple drafts, is like climbing a mountain. I'm not sure why I think this is a good analogy because I have never climbed a mountain, and I'm pretty sure none of my students have either, but I feel like it works when I am breaking the news that the work they have invested has generally not led to the increase in points they expected. I tell them that writing does not follow a simple equation, as in x amount of work always leads to x amount of success. When we write, like when climbing a mountain, there are diminishing returns. Doubling the amount of work and time it took to write a C paper does not automatically lead to an A paper.

I tell my students (all my understanding of the topic based on a couple readings of *Into Thin Air*) that it's relatively easy to get to base camp on Mount Everest. With the right guides, people can get there with training done on lunches and weekends at the YMCA. But this is where the real work begins, when the diminishing returns begin. Because the air is thinner near the top, the terrain is steeper and more challenging. It simply takes more work to travel the same distance that was relatively easy at the start of the climb. Obviously, students want to climb as quickly during the revision process as they have earlier, but it doesn't work that way. Sometimes they even have to go backwards, abandon the path they are on, and find a new, more promising one. I tell them I will be their Sherpa, if they need me, if they choose to keep climbing to get an A. But I also tell them that even the Sherpa, though experienced, needs to create each climb anew. Because the mountain and conditions are always changing. I say to them, "I can see the path you are on and can envision the path you can take to get to the top. It can be done. You can get there. I can help. But just because it can be done doesn't mean it will be easy or that either of us know exactly how to do it or how long it will take."

Another way I have led my students to make a connection to help them learn about the nuts and bolts of writing is to have them compare the draft of a paper to a football team. Luckily, I teach in Wisconsin, home of the Green Bay Packers, and the Packers are always a topic of conversation in the fall semester. So sometimes when we read a sample essay, or do peer review, I'll tell them to imagine the draft they are reading is like the offensive squad on football— whose goal is to gain yards and score points. I'll let my students know what equates to a first down (a good thesis statement or topic sentence), what amounts to a long gain (a fresh comparison or specific example that really highlights the point the writer is making and entertains the reader). I tell them to award touchdowns and field goals, note turnovers (for example, a misinterpretation of one of the source writer's ideas) and penalties (spelling, grammar, punctuation, et cetera). This has proven to be a fun, effective way (best in small groups) to have them respond to a work in progress by connecting it to something they already know. It's fun for them, and without realizing it, they are making a connection and using a critical lens to analyze a piece of writing.

6. Take advantage of the desire to produce

Another thing that should help keep your students engaged in their work is the fact that in composition class, unlike many of the other classes they'll be taking, they get to *produce* something. This satisfies a natural human urge, and you should take advantage of it. You can even point this out to them, the fact that while in other classes they may solve problems, learn techniques, or be exposed to new information, when they write, they are *making* something—something new, unique, important. Especially as first-year students, I don't think they are creating too many original works in history class, calculus, biology, psychology. They are learning in those classes, but all solving the same problems, all learning the same information. They are not creating anything new. But in our classes, that's exactly what they should be doing.

I've already talked about the kinds of writing assignments that work best at the onset of the semester, but before too much time passes, you've got to get them started on academic writing—the kind the school has hired you to teach them. In my experience, each department has had clearly stated goals for each class, but it is often up to the teacher to determine how to get their students there by the end of the semester. The assignment sequence is the key to helping your students accomplish their goals by the end of the semester. Every assignment should be crafted with the end goals in mind. And to keep students invested, they need to be working on authentic tasks. Everything they do should be real work and matter to them. Students know when they are given busy work that doesn't lead to anything, and they'll rightly rebel in one form or another. To prevent this, I try to give my students only assignments and exercises that I, with lots more experience writing and learning, would benefit from. I know if this is true, the assignment is equally or more valuable for them.

7. Help them find their thesis

A key to getting students to produce something worthwhile and satisfying (to them as writers) is getting them to the point where they know what they want to say sooner rather than later. This doesn't mean rushing the process or telling them what to say, but helping them understand the process of discovering what they want to say. This process varies from writer to writer: some need to write to discover their ideas, others find this through discussion, reading, or silent contemplation. But the sooner they have a clear plan, the better the writing is, both in terms of the process (for them) and in terms of the product (for readers).

Here's a version of the handout I use:

- -

A thesis statement:

- States your argument (your position on a topic + your reasons)
- Serves as a "road map" for the paper, previewing the organization of your essay
- Directly answers the question asked of you (even if you're not given a question, think of your thesis as an answer to a question)
- Makes a claim that others might dispute
- Is 1-2 sentences long and is presented at the end of the introduction (end of your first paragraph)

How do you get a thesis?

A thesis is often the result of a lengthy thinking process, and formulating a thesis is typically not the first part of the writing process. This is because before you develop an argument on any topic, you have to think about the topic, write about the topic, collect and organize evidence, look for possible relationships between known facts (such as surprising contrasts or similarities), and think about the significance of these relationships. Once you do this, you will probably have a "working thesis," a basic or main idea, an argument that you think you can support with evidence but will become more developed throughout the writing process.

How do you know if your thesis is strong?

When reviewing your first draft and its working thesis, ask yourself the following:

- *Am I answering the question?* Think of your thesis as an answer to a question, so even if the assignment sheet does not pose a question, create your own based on the subject.
- *Is my position one that others might oppose?* If your thesis simply states facts that no one would disagree with, you are not making an argument.
- *Is my thesis statement specific enough?* If your thesis contains vague words like "good" or "successful," be more specific: *why* is something "good"; *what* makes something "successful"?

- ***Does my thesis pass the "So what?" test?*** If a reader's first response is "So what?" then you need to clarify, connect to a larger issue, or lead the reader to care about your position in some other way.
- ***Does my thesis pass the "How?" and "Why?" tests?*** If a reader's first response is "How?" or "Why?" your thesis is too open-ended.

(Adapted from: https://writingcenter.unc.edu/tips-and-tools/thesis-statements/)

- -

I have found that the sooner students are able to write a clear, well-developed thesis statement, the easier the semester becomes (for both them and for you). My students work on this frequently early in the semester. For some, it may become redundant, but lots of them come into the semester thinking the thesis statement should be like a "coming attractions" preview at the movie theater—a teaser, a little hint of what to expect. Others think it's just a clear preview of the topics that will be discussed. (In this paper I will . . .) No, I tell them. The thesis statement needs to clearly state your position, with reasons that don't leave your reader asking how or why questions. Lots of them say to me, "Who will want to read my paper if I tell them what I'm going to say? If I give it all away?" What makes a paper interesting, I explain, is not just *having* an argument, it's having an *interesting, compelling* argument and *explaining* and *supporting* that argument. It's taking your reader on the journey of discovery you have traveled to write the paper.

I tell my students that once they have a good, clear thesis statement, the task of writing the paper becomes much easier. They know what to say, what to leave out, and in what order to present ideas. As you surely know, papers written without a clear thesis tend to ramble off topic, fail to gain traction or say anything clearly. Students who turn in papers like this often tell me they are disappointed with them. And frustrated. Writing a paper like this is like trying to navigate without a rudder. Luckily, there is usually something that can be salvaged. Often, papers written like this arrive at a thesis statement in the concluding paragraph. When this happens, I tell them they should be happy, that they needed to write the draft they've written to *find* the thesis statement. I tell them that is the way a lot of writers operate.

"But now I need to rewrite the paper?" they ask.

"No," I tell them. "You have to *keep writing* it."

To facilitate their appreciation of thesis statements, I spend parts of two or three classes early in the semester working on them. One day we'll discuss what a thesis statement is, what it needs to do, and look at examples of good thesis statements. I'll give them a series of questions to choose from, and each group answers one in the form of a thesis statement (with clear reasons why they have taken the position they have). Here's what I'll give them (or show them) for that exercise:

- -

Write a thesis statement in response to one of the following questions. Provide at least 3 reasons to support your position:

- Who is the best quarterback in the NFL today?
- Who is more important for college students' success: friends or family?
- Should the government restrict the sale of unhealthy foods?
- Should attendance count towards semester grades in college?
- Should people be allowed to keep pit bulls as pets?
- Should a literature class be required for all college students?
- Should college students be Facebook friends with their parents?

- -

Then I say (ideally, this is about fifteen minutes before class is scheduled to end), "No one gets out of here without a good thesis statement!" Sometimes I sweeten the deal: either write a good thesis statement, taking a position on the topic with at least three valid reasons supporting it, or your homework will be to write a three-page essay on the topic before next class. They always come up with (sometimes with my help) a solid thesis statement before the end of class.

Now the questions I just listed are relatively simple, so students end up writing relatively simple thesis statements, much less complex than the ones they will need to write for their papers during the semester. But what I want them to do is learn how to write a thesis statement that presents an argument, with reasons. And as a result of these exercises, instead of thesis statements like "Genetic Engineering: Ethical or Not?", I've had students write thesis statements like these:

> *Cliques are capable of preventing the discovery of the individual self and postponing success in adult life. Adolescents need good role models in their immediate families and solid moral foundations to combat the negative effects from pseudomature behaviors and conformity encouraged by their peers in cliques.*

> *Gender stereotypes, whether or not they are intentional, are very prevalent in comic books, and these stereotypes, in addition to marginalizing and underrepresenting women, are detrimental to female readers as they decrease egalitarian gender role beliefs and lower body esteem.*

These are both examples from students of mine who entered (and were selected as winners of) our annual Research Paper Contest (which is another good way to motivate your strongest students to keep revising and improving).

8. Craft inviting assignment sheets

The assignment sheets you give to students should not only clearly spell out the objectives of the assignment, they should also be used as a motivational tool. People like to be challenged, so use language that activates this desire. You can present the assignment like a puzzle to be solved or an invitation to connect a new idea to an existing debate. I like to leave my assignment sheets somewhat open-ended so students don't feel like they are just "meeting the requirements." I'll clearly state the goals for the assignment, but also let them know that there are unlimited ways to get there, unlimited possibilities. I have found that if I leave room in the assignment parameters for creativity and discovery, that's what will happen.

Though your department will surely provide a list of learning objectives and outcomes for your students, and your goal is to help your students learn how to meet them, avoid including these on the assignment sheets, in their formal language, that is. Few students will get excited when told to write a paper that "demonstrates the ability to situate the writer's perspective in relation to that of texts under consideration" or "provides analyses with reasoning and evidence appropriate to the content."

In a way, I always have two assignment sheets: one for the student and one for me. The assignment sheet I begin with is for me only—it clearly states what I want them to do for an assignment and explains how it fits with the learning objectives for the class. For example, I may want them to *construct an argument on a topic that uses another writer's ideas as a critical lens.* Then I use that to craft the assignment sheet for them—written in a way to get them invested. Such as: "Based on Susan Engel's ideas about how autobiographical memories are essential for one's selfhood, write a paper that answers the following question: if a person lost all memories, would this person have the same self, a different self, or somewhere in between?" If you recall, I mentioned this earlier as a class discussion topic. Sometimes I use it that way, other times as a formal paper. How do I decide? Sometimes I know ahead of time, but it is based on how they responded to the discussion question. If there was a lively debate and it feels like we could have kept going, I might make it a paper topic. If I feel like most of the important, interesting things have already been said, we won't go back to it.

However I decide on the topic for the papers, I want them to see themselves as exploring and digging into ideas. I want them to read about these ideas, understand them, put them in some sort of context, relating them to other ideas and to themselves. I want them to speculate: "What if this? Why is that?" I want them to see hidden connections, come up with their own connections, engage in the kind of thinking and discovery that makes writing so magical. And that's how I want them to think of it, as a quest, an act of discovery, the process of finding different meanings and seeing how they speak to each other. I want them coming through the process more informed, aware, and interested in the topic, with something to say. I don't want my students to be thinking: "Tomorrow morning, I'm going to wake up early, clear my mind, and sit down to,

'Provide analyses with reasoning and evidence appropriate to the content.'" Because, let's face it, that is nothing to get excited about.

If you look back at the assignment sheet for the Analysis of "Self-Reliance" paper, that is the level of detail I will provide eventually. But usually I will have them start by simply responding to questions (in response to readings) such as:

> Compare your experiences at prom with the argument that prom is not only a waste of money, but that it promotes narcissism and self-indulgence.

> If Ralph Waldo Emerson and Friedrich Nietzsche had a long discussion on the idea of the individual, what would they say to each other? On what points would they agree? Disagree? Why?

> Emerson says self-reliance is the key to one's best life. But Roy Baumeister says people have taken this too far and become selfish and narcissistic. Based on your experiences and observations, is Baumeister correct? Is it possible to be self-reliant without being narcissistic?

> How does social media use affect adolescents, particularly regarding self-esteem, empathy, and/or friendships?

These kinds of questions lead to them accomplishing the goals for the class, but their tasks are presented as something to be genuinely interested in. They'll be focused on *saying something*, not simply engaging in one or another form of academic discourse. As Sholem Asch said, "Writing is a lot easier if you have something to say."

If an assignment is to be informal and ungraded, the assignment sheet should reflect that. But for graded papers, which by their nature are more important, it needs to be more clear. It may seem that my assignment sheet for the Analysis of "Self-Reliance" is too prescriptive. But I have found that even with these clear instructions, students are always surprising me with the ways they *don't* follow directions. Some will submit rambling, incoherent personal essays that don't mention Emerson at all. Others will write *only* about Emerson and not even start to create their own arguments, as if they haven't read the full assignment sheet. But the students that do follow these instructions will meet the objectives *and* create something new, something that matters to them. Lots of students agree with Emerson and discuss their own experiences of conforming to others. Some discuss others' inability to be self-reliant and the damage it did to them. Some students disagree because they argue self-reliance ignores the importance of God, or because they think society needs a clear hierarchy to function. One student disagreed with his argument because she felt she had learned important things from role models in her life and Emerson seemed to be dismissing the value of them (and look, she also took that idea and turned it into a contest-winning research paper!). I don't care what they've got to say, as long as they have *something* to say. And I don't think they have to know that they are demonstrating "the ability to situate the writer's perspective in relation to that of texts under consideration" or providing "analyses with reasoning and evidence appropriate to the content." I know that that is what they are doing, and that's what is important.

9. Have them share their discoveries

Another good strategy to help students get invested is to have them share their ideas and paper topics with the rest of the class. This is especially valuable when they are still at the point when they are considering what to write about. For example, after we've read Plato's "Allegory of the Cave" and I tell them they need to analyze a group in contemporary society that is in some sort of cave, blinded to reality, I will have them all share what group they plan to write about, whether it's the Amish, Republicans, suburbanites, or supermodels. Some will want to hold their topics back, figuring it's better to wow everyone with their brilliance when they bring their drafts to peer review, but don't let them. Each idea discussed, good or bad, will spark something in all the other students' minds and ultimately lead to better topics for everyone. As Linus Pauling said, "The best way to have a good idea is to have lots of ideas."

Another reason why this is valuable is because often as students try to explain their topics, they will see the flaws in them. For example, if someone's research question begins as "What are the arguments for and against human cloning?", I can say that's a good topic but a bad question. Because it could be answered in a simple report, with none of the writer's own ideas. I'll suggest a better question: "Is human cloning ethical?" Now the student needs to define ethics and take a stand on the issue, say something beyond just what the sources say. Eventually, the topic will get narrower and more interesting. I tell my students the most interesting papers (to read and to write) are those that focus very narrowly on part of a topic, then go as in-depth as possible once inside the topic, like they have to squeeze themselves through a narrow opening and then see what's inside.

Here's another simple example: If a student wants to write about "The benefits of sports participation for children," that would probably end up an overly simplistic "report." But if the student discusses the benefits of sports participation as part of an argument that says, "Students should be required to participate in sports because . . ." then the writer needs to take a much more active role, considering topics like the rights of the individual, considering other compulsory things (education and vaccinations) and the whole idea of rules, regulations, and requirements. I mean, the government has a say in telling people what they can and cannot do, based on both what is good for the individual and society as a whole, so why shouldn't something like sports participation, if it is proven to be valuable, be required? Military service is required in some countries. Vaccinations in others. Why not track and field? I tell my students the best papers are those that bring in ideas from a lot of different places—politics, psychology, popular culture, et cetera. My point here is that talking with the class about all the possible ways to look at topics will help all the other students see how to frame their own questions so they can write about the topics they are interested in, but do so in a compelling way.

10. Make them accountable to the reader

Another way to keep your students engaged in their work is to remind them that they have readers and that with every piece of writing they produce, they are entering into a sort of contract with those readers. Tell them that reading is at its essence a matter of giving up one's time, one's mind, to whatever one is reading. Tell them that reading properly means doing nothing else (as you can see, this is also good advice to make them better readers). Tell them that life is made up of time, that every minute is precious, and that every time one picks up a book, an article, a poem, even a paper written for a composition class, this reader is essentially saying: "I am freely giving up my time, part of my life (my life!) to read what you've written." If they know this is what their readers are investing, they'll be more likely to invest the time and effort needed to write well.

You should also be, as early as possible, making them aware of what their readers need, what kind of background information, what kind of explanations. Awareness of audience is key to growing as a writer because even though having control of one's own thoughts comes first, lots of what we write needs to be communicated to others. But here I am talking about having empathy for their readers, not just intellectually, but in all ways. Let your student know what Samuel Johnson said, that is, "What is written without effort is generally read without pleasure." Whatever else they want out of life, very few want to produce unpleasurable experiences for others.

Making It Through the Semester Without Burning Out

If you are unsure about adopting some of these strategies and changing the way you teach, remember that all my advice is not only geared towards maximizing your students' success—it is for your benefit too. I know you've got a life, plans and goals, things to do. Whether it's to run a marathon, write a book, or learn a foreign language, you're surely up to something. And you don't want your teaching to burn you out, which can happen very easily if you teach with a confrontational attitude, if you engage in ill-conceived, self-destructive warfare with your students. Sun Tzu says, "One who is skilled in warfare principles subdues the enemy without doing battle, takes the enemy's walled city without attacking, and overthrows the enemy quickly, without protracted warfare." In other words, you can achieve victory, meet your objectives, help your students learn to be better writers, all without sacrificing yourself.

How does one do this? Well, aside from what I've already explained, Sun Tzu's advice is "If it is not advantageous, do not move." This means don't work just for work's sake. Don't keep yourself busy just for the sake of keeping busy. Everything you do should have a clear, important objective. If it doesn't, it's probably a waste of energy (both yours and your students'). I've explained how to use the peer review process to maximize your students' work (and learning) while minimizing yours. By planning well, you can create weeks of the semester when your students will all be busy working and you won't. Don't feel guilty about this. You'll invest plenty of energy along the way.

Always keep in mind the desired outcome of the work. Ask yourself, what advantage can I gain? Then, what do I need to do to gain that advantage? If you teach the day's lesson and your strategy is not working, try something else. If that doesn't work, you may need to stop for the day, figure out a new strategy. There's always a way. Of course, whether you are abandoning a goal for the day, or if you have met it ahead of schedule, you should always have something else for your students to do. The time you have together is essential.

At the same time, sometimes when your class has performed well, when your objectives have been met and the next one can't be met in the amount of class time left, let them go early. Only ask them to invest time if something can be accomplished. Don't start something if you'll just have to start it over again next class. Never rush through anything. Sometimes—not often, but sometimes—just let them go. Students love getting out of class ten minutes early because those minutes, when one is unexpectedly free, even for students who enjoy class, are magical; they take on a special quality, like waking up refreshed from a great night's sleep on a beautiful spring day—happy, happy.

And besides the fact that you can give them this special treat, which they will appreciate, when you let them go early sometimes, it reinforces the idea that all the minutes you do spend in the classroom together are important. They'll know in your class they'll never be wasting their time.

Sun Tzu also says, "When doing battle, seek a quick victory." That is, though the preparation and training may have to be extensive, the actual battles should be quick. For our purposes, think of these "battles" as the interactions (between you and your students and your students with each other) needed to accomplish the goals along the way. The key is to prepare well ahead of time, anticipate their responses, and direct their energy in productive directions. Sometimes, a bit of struggle is needed to help them reach the objective (finding common ground between two seemingly disconnected ideas, for example). Sometimes a long, twisted road is the best road, but often it isn't. Again, always think of the end point, the goal, and the experiences you want them to have throughout the process, then plan the easiest, most efficient path to get them there. Learning to write well is challenging enough without you trying to make it more difficult.

Sun Tzu also says, "If troops lay siege to a walled city, their strength will be exhausted." First, you can think of your students as "the troops," and while it's important they work hard, you don't want to "exhaust" them by, for example, as discussed earlier, reading impenetrable essays, then withholding advice and guidance. They'll be exhausted before they've learned a thing, and as a result will probably tune you out. You also don't want to give them too much work. Composition class, though surely the most important, is only one of many classes they'll be taking, and requiring too much output inevitably results in lower quality, which only means you'll need to redouble your efforts. Less material can often lead to more learning because assigning too much is asking for superficial responses. Obviously, there needs to be a minimum number of pages for the semester. They'll learn to write by writing. But it's also true that they'll learn to write well by writing well. If someone wanted to become a better free throw shooter, if that was this person's main goal for the summer, some people might advise him or her to shoot five hundred free throws per day. But that wouldn't do much good if one was doing it wrong, with bad form, with feet in the wrong place, without properly flicking the wrist and following through. More beneficial for this player would be to *make* one hundred free throws, with good form, doing it the right way. It's the same for writing. Less can be more. And if you make it easier for them to write well, it is easier for you because it's easier to grade better work.

As for minimum page requirements, I always have a number in mind, but I tell my students that the numbers I suggest are the ones needed to accomplish the goals of the assignment. Let them know that the number of pages or words you are asking for are based on what the assignment is asking them to do, not just an arbitrary number. Though some will try to skimp as the process unfolds, through early drafts, peer review, conferences, and grades, they'll see why the paper needs to be the lengths you have indicated.

The second way to look at that quote is to see yourself as "the troops" whose strength you don't want exhausted. This goes back to what I've already said. You've got limitations. You won't be a good teacher if you don't have energy, so plan the course to make the best use of what you've got. No matter how ambitious or dedicated you are, you must realize there are walls you will not be able to scale in a semester. Not all your students will dazzle you by the end of the term. Be realistic and set attainable goals for what you can accomplish in a semester. If you push your students straight into very difficult tasks, they'll fail, and you'll get frustrated. It would be like if you were a track coach and had your runners do a race on the first day of the season, after a long, cold winter in which none of them have been training enough. Not only would they fail to run good times, some would hurt themselves trying, and they'd get angry at you for putting them in that position. Just like an athlete's, a writer's skills need to be developed gradually and with a mix of stimuli: hard days, easy days, drills, recovery, days off, stretching, et cetera.

Sun Tzu also says, "If the army is exposed to a prolonged campaign, the nation's resources will not suffice." Think of yourself as the army here and, again, consider your limitations. Sure, you are a composition teacher, but you are still human, and you need sleep, time for your other classes, time for yourself, your family, friends, pets. You need to be able to wake up some days feeling fresh and optimistic, sometimes with nothing to do. That's right, you should have whole days, sometimes whole weekends, with nothing to do, when you won't think once about your

composition class. This is important because once you've
burned yourself out, there's no coming back, there's just
hanging on until the end of the semester, and your teaching and your students will suffer.

Because what happens when you are burned out? Well,
Sun Tzu says, "When weapons are blunted and ardor
dampened, strength exhausted and resources depleted,
the neighboring rulers will take advantage of these com-
plications." That is to say, if you are not sharp, you'll lose
control. The "neighboring rulers" you need to be afraid
of are simply bad writing, bad work habits, bad attitudes,
laziness, complacency, sloppy thinking, et cetera. Your
students can also be seen as the "neighboring rulers," and
yes, even after you've primed them for success all semester,
if you give them the chance to take the easy way out, lots
of them will take it. How will you know if you're getting
burned out? Well, if you find yourself getting angry at your
students, resentful of your colleagues or anyone in your
life, or if you think about class and conclude that you or
your students "just don't care," then you're in trouble.

The way to avoid this is to save your energy for what really matters, the things you need to do. For your own sake,
don't grade everything they write. For some things, don't
even write down comments besides maybe a quick note
at the end so they know you've read it. The key is to get
them writing. Of course, they need some sense of how well
they've accomplished the goals of the assignment. As I've
already explained, the method that saves time here is to
read and discuss sample responses—make copies of one or
two of their papers, read them aloud in class, and discuss

them. This allows you and the class to discover and discuss strengths and weaknesses (the same strengths and weaknesses found in most of their papers) in one tenth of the time. They'll take what they learn in the class discussion of someone else's paper and see how to best apply it to their own writing. So when they do submit papers for grades, they'll be that much better and that much easier for you to grade. This time-saving strategy is important because there are some things you'll go to great, great lengths to teach, some things you'll need to spend lots of time and energy on, but you can't do this for everything.

One thing you'll need to spend a lot of time on is grading major assignments. There really is no way around it—you are going to spend a lot of time. Ideally, you'll even read things twice, reading over papers once closely and writing down notes and suggestions in the margins, then going back and reading over it again as you fill out the rubric. The reason to do it this way is that often, for example, it does you no good to comment or assign points for the thesis statement before you see whether or not the paper follows through on it. At the end of the process, it's best to write a thoughtful paragraph or two along with the grade—re-emphasizing the paper's strengths and weaknesses. Whenever possible, include positive comments on papers—I always write "good topic sentence" or "good example," even if I was the one to suggest it to the student. Part of your job is to help your students identify what good writing is, and they won't always pick up on this as quickly as you'd like them to. Always grade papers and write comments as if students will revise, even though they may choose not to. Point to opportunities where the paper can go further and really succeed. In my classes, I allow revisions for all papers because, especially for developing writers, revision is the key to writing, and I believe that not allowing it is not really teaching them how to write. I've already explained that assignment sheets with clear objectives will make their papers better, and you should also give them the rubric before they write the papers so they know exactly what they'll be graded on. Grading papers will probably be the hardest, most time-consuming part of your job, but there's no way around it. Plan for it, find a process that works for you, and make sure you have the energy to do it without getting burned out.

Though I have gotten better at grading papers on my computer, and I like having a record of them available for both me and the students and having access to all drafts, if I have the time, I still prefer to get (or print) paper copies, take them to an empty desk or chair, someplace with minimal distractions, and just work through them, one at a time, of course. If I've got a stack of twenty, I may stop after five and get up and stretch my legs. "Five more," I'll tell myself, "and I'll be halfway done." Then I'll break these last ten into smaller groups of four, four, and two, because it's easier for me this way, like when I'm doing a long run, it's easier to break into pieces, landmarks, where I can give myself a little pat on the back for getting to where I have gotten. Sometimes I have to go back because I graded the first papers differently than the rest. Yes, there are objective requirements, but it's also easier to assess how strong one student's paper is after you've read a number of them.

But even if I have to backtrack like this, I always keep looking ahead, ahead to the finish, ah yes, and then it happens, somehow it always happens, when I get to the point where I have no more papers to grade. "I've done it," I think. "I've finished. Good job!" Then I remind myself, "That was only one section. You've got two more." "Tomorrow," I say, and I don't think one bit about it until I start again the next day, another stack of twenty in my lap, and then another twenty the day after that. "It's hard work," I tell myself, "but all for the greater good."

Because there's so much progress to be made, and so little time to do it, you may try to hurry. But Sun Tzu says that "rolling up your armor, rushing forward without stopping day or night, covering twice the distance" will only lead to defeat. That is, if you move too quickly, assigning papers in quick succession, flying through a discussion on active and passive voice, only the strongest students will be able to keep up, and you may not even be teaching them anything new or anything they couldn't have figured out on their own. To hurry through something important is to waste everyone's time. Always remember composition is a class where success is based on quality, not quantity. If your students can write one very good paper at the end of the semester, assuming they couldn't beforehand, you have succeeded.

Another way to preserve yourself is to, as Sun Tzu says, "Take equipment from home but take provisions from the enemy" or "feed off the enemy." This means you'll bring the expertise, knowledge, and tools needed to improve writing—but you'll let your students bring the energy, the ideas. Though they may not always appear this way, they've got lots of energy, or at least potential energy, and are full of ideas, questions, opinions, et cetera. Even with all their angst and confusion and ego, or maybe because of it, they've each got at least as much potential energy than you, and if there are twenty of them in the class, that is more than enough energy to fuel the semester. Don't let them sit and store it up for something else. The key, of course, is to draw it out of them, ask questions, force them to answer: "How has your life been affected by gender roles, or family, or privilege (or lack of it)?" Or to make it simpler: "What would you do if you had one year left to live? How about one week?" As explained earlier, even if your students have discussed these in class, ask for answers in writing. It's a writing class, after all. And what they write is often more interesting than what they say in class, and you can read these back the next day (anonymously) to start up some even better class discussions on these topics.

Also remember that energy begets energy, so if you've got students with things to say, who come to class ready to engage, speak, even if they are not your best or brightest, let them go, let them talk. Ideas are infectious too, good and bad, no idea stands alone. Think of your students as twenty pieces of kindling—they can get hot, they can burn, but they need to be arranged properly, and you've got to figure out where the spark is coming from to get the fire started.

Discipline and Reward

In a perfect world, all your students would be fully invested and eager to do the work. But the composition class does not exist in a perfect world, it exists in our world, and so you'll need to think about other ways to motivate your students. Sun Tzu says an effective leader needs to "command with benevolence and unify them by discipline." I have already talked about your benevolence and ways to unify students. But you need your students to see themselves not only as a group, but as members of a group that wants to succeed. And if you really want your students to succeed, you must not only convey high standards and express confidence that students can meet them, you need to make sure there are consequences when they don't.

One of the most obvious ways to do this is through grading. This is often at the top of the minds of your students at the beginning of the semester: "What grade can I get in this course?" However, if you are like me, I expect that grades are one of the last things you are thinking about as the semester begins. Instead, I am asking: "How can I teach these people to be better writers?" In my classes, I under-emphasize grades (until the end of the semester at least) for a few reasons. First, as I have already explained, studies have shown that people are more motivated when they are focused on intrinsic rewards instead of extrinsic. This means if students are writing just for grades, they are not as motivated as they'd be if they were writing to discover ideas, to clearly express their thoughts, to learn and grow. That's what I try to get them focused on.

Sometimes I think it would be nice if there were no grades in composition class, if it was like a great writing group, with long conversations about writing and everyone doing multiple drafts, eagerly engaged in extensive revisions, always paying attention to detail, just because that's the way it should be done. But it won't happen that way. And because grades matter to your students, you need to use them to your advantage. And if you feel sheepish about this for some reason, like it's not in your nature to be judgmental, remember what your objective is, helping your students learn to write and learn The Way. And fair grading not only helps motivate them, but clearly communicates with them the extent to which they are succeeding (or not). If you want to take teaching seriously, you've got to take grading seriously as well.

The first thing I do when discussing grades is convince them that my goal, like theirs, is that they get good grades. I explain we are working towards this goal together, that I am there to help, not oppose, them on their quest to succeed. I've found it's easier to convince them of this when I've taught at schools that have a portfolio review process, where students' writing is measured against the course goals, anonymously, by other instructors, and those instructors determine which papers meet the goals, essentially determining whether students pass the course or will need to repeat it. I like this structure because it makes it clear to students that the teacher is there to help. But even if there is not a portfolio review process in place at your school, you can still show them that this is the nature of your relationship. The key is to be as transparent and objective as possible when grading. Go out of your way to make it clear that *you* are not the one determining the grade, you are simply a witness to the performance the student provides, a third-party observer, noting the ways in which the assignment meets or fails to meet its objectives, just like if you were grading a multiple-choice quiz. Of course, it's not as simple as that. Reading and grading is tough, complicated work that takes a lot of energy no matter how one does it. And it takes even more work to do it in a way that shows your students you are being objective, but this is what you need to do. Because if they don't pay attention to your comments and the grades, they won't learn to become better writers.

Because of the nature of composition class (learning to write), I believe grades should be based on what students can do at the end of the semester. That's why a final portfolio (whether read just by you or by others) that accounts for a large percentage of the grade is a good idea. Allowing or requiring students to revise graded assignments is also a great way to keep them invested and improving. Whenever possible, I try to show them that revision is the key to writing. If I have them, I'll hand out sample papers from previous semesters—an early draft and a final draft—so they can see what a full-scale revision looks like, see that it's not just editing and "fixing mistakes." If I don't have a good example of something I want to show them, I'll write one myself. I'll write a bad two-page essay and then revise and write a better one (not too good though, as I don't want to blow my cover).

Sometimes I even talk about how I labored over an assignment sheet, discuss early drafts that just didn't quite work, saying, "I was going to give you this other version, but it just wasn't good enough—you deserved better." In the syllabus and with each assignment sheet, you need to make the evaluation and grading criteria clear. *What* will be graded? *How* will it be graded? *Why* will it be graded that way? They need to know the answers to all these questions. If you give them a set of goals that are achievable and clearly explain what needs to be done to reach these goals, you can grade with a clear conscience and "punish" the students who don't perform well.

But this can be tricky because, as Sun Tzu says, "If one punishes the troops before their loyalty is formed, they will be disobedient." This is why it is important to have formed bonds with them, exhibiting your compassion and generosity, getting to know them, before you give out any grades. This way, when you "punish" them (with grades lower than they want), they'll know why you're doing it—only to help them. It will be clear that you are not out to get them or setting them up or tricking them into failure. They'll know you have given an honest, objective assessment of their work. Moreover, they should get the sense that their low grades hurt you in the same way it hurts them (and to an extent, this should be true). If you have been clear in the assignment goals and shown you genuinely want them to succeed, they will accept the grades they get as accurate reflections of their work, not personal indictments, and will be motivated to improve.

Sun Tzu goes on to say, "If one does not punish the troops after their loyalty is formed, they cannot be used." This means once you've established yourself as a credible, benevolent leader, you need to follow through on your threats—you need to give them bad grades if that's what they've earned, you've got to penalize them for turning in work late, for missing class, et cetera. Once you've clearly established what it takes to succeed in the class and shown them that their success is your goal, you've got to "punish" them when they don't perform. If you don't, they'll just tune you out and never learn.

Also, when grading, or whenever you give feedback on written assignments, it must focus on the work: the writing, the content, how well the documents they submit to you are meeting the goals. The language you use is important, and though your students may not seem all that sophisticated when it comes to language, they'll pick up on all sorts of nuances and read into your comments in the ways you would wish they'd read into everything. So be sure to always critique the writing, never the student; don't say, for example, "You are not being clear here." Instead, say, "This sentence is not clear." Don't say, "Your ideas are messy." Instead, say, "The organization of ideas in this draft needs to be improved." Earlier, I said the way to get students invested in their work was to get them to understand that everything they write is a personal reflection on them, a way to transfer the very essence of their beings to others. And while I'm not going to take that back, as it is important that they see it that way, when you are critiquing and commenting on student work, these two things (the student and the work) must be kept separate. When you read and grade papers, think of the writing as existing separate from the person and address it in this way. Read it and grade it as if you don't know the student because that's what writing needs to do—communicate clearly, provide all necessary background information, capture the essence of the writer in one way or another. "Don't think of me as your reader," I tell them. "Imagine what you have written is being blown along by the wind one day, and someone stops to pick it up, a total stranger. Will that reader understand what you are trying to say?" The answer should be yes.

You also need to make it clear to your students that the value of a piece of writing—to the reader, that is—is not dependent upon how much work the writer has put in. You'll likely hear a lot about how hard some of your students have worked and their belief that this should guarantee them a good grade. You'll need to explain to them that while you appreciate that they may have worked hard (and maybe they really did), the writing, the final product they submit, is what matters for the grade. It is what it is, and if it doesn't do what it needs to do, you need to say so, and they need to know it.

Another good rule to keep in mind for grading is that no matter how tired or frustrated you may get when grading a stack of papers, remember that flaws in the writing are not flaws in the person. You will see the flaws in the writing, but stop there. Because neither you nor your students will benefit when you get angry with them or make assumptions about anything else. And though you may think you are able to hide this from your students, they'll sense it, they'll know it, just like you know when someone is frustrated with you. This is not the relationship you want to have with them. Keep in mind what Saint Augustine (or maybe it was Gandhi) said: "Hate the sin, love the sinner."

Sun Tzu's rule is: "In chariot battles, reward the first to capture at least ten chariots." We can relate this to the nice thing about grading—the fact that you get to reward students who do the work, who meet the goals, and write good papers. If a student really earns an A on a paper, not only does that make your job easier, it's a real joy to be the bearer of that good news.

Because grades are private, unless students decide to share their grades with their classmates, you can't quite use those as motivation. But there are other ways to reward students that can not only bolster those students, but help motivate all others in the class. It's important to reward students who show initiative, serve as class leaders, and have strong writing skills in ways that not only affirm the value of their efforts but also encourage others to strive for more. However, it's tricky because you don't want to display too much adulation, especially early in the semester, as this can separate those students from the rest of the class and encourage resentment, as skeptics and strugglers will be more resistant to both you and the strong students. So you must be subtle in the classroom, putting the strong students in the position to exhibit their skills, interests, and curiosity for the rest of the class. But you must do this without it seeming like you are doing this, like it is happening naturally. I mean, it does occur naturally, but to help make it occur more often, sometimes you have got to help nature out.

For example, you might lead a full-class discussion after watching excerpts from the latest political debate, and you might lead the discussion right up to the key point, where you might want to say, "And this is where our dear President is guilty of the logical fallacy of circular reasoning." But instead of *you* saying this, if you can get one of your students to say it, you are much better off. The point you wanted to make will be clear to the class, and the student who made the key statement will feel great for being able to put into words an idea one's whole group has been building towards or struggling with. It's one of the experiences in life that creates a feeling of real buoyancy. And all the other students don't just benefit from the content, what has been said, they also benefit from seeing the process, seeing their classmate find the right answer. They will want to experience that for themselves and will be more engaged in future discussions. In the end, you've gotten your point across to the class, the student is rewarded (and others are motivated), but no one else in the class thinks you have done the rewarding.

Another way to reward students is by asking small groups to complete a task in response to a question you've posed and then have them write their answers on the board and discuss their relative merits. Some groups will do better than others, and if you are leading the discussion properly, all the groups should be able to identify the stronger responses. Again, those who have succeeded at the exercise, who have "captured ten chariots," will be rewarded, this time by acknowledgment of their success and by their peers' approval, which is equally, and for some a more important, motivating factor. But it won't seem like you are playing favorites. The material being judged is up on the board for everyone to see. You are just an objective observer.

When writing comments on papers, of course, you can be more complimentary. You can also voice your satisfaction with a job well done when the class is discussing anonymous student papers. Of course, it's important not to praise the writer, but the work, pointing out that being clear, going beyond the obvious, taking the reader's needs into consideration, supporting claims, et cetera, are the keys to successful writing. The class as a whole will be focused on the paper, but the anonymous student you are praising will be feeling good about the paper's success, and others will aspire to meet this performance with their own work.

Sometimes you can "reward" students more obviously in the classroom in a way that doesn't build resentment. For example, a few times during the semester, I'll give students (or sometimes groups) an in-class exercise and say when they complete it, to my satisfaction, they earn an early dismissal from class. Now the assignments that lead to this kind of reward shouldn't be based on preexisting abilities because students bring different levels of expertise to the class, and to reward students simply for being stronger writers at the beginning of the semester can have negative consequences, building resentment and breaking up the team mentality while simultaneously discouraging weaker students and giving the stronger ones too much credit. So individual assignments that can earn a student an early exit from class are best if their success is dependent upon either paying attention in class or preparing for class as instructed.

For example, some days I'll ask my students to bring in a rough draft of a paper and then ask them to write a sentence outline in class. This is more developed than a topic outline because they must write a complete sentence summing up the main point of each paragraph, essentially creating a topic sentence for each paragraph. It's a great way to get them to see how their paper is organized, and if a student has a solid draft written, with good topic sentences already in place, producing the outline should be relatively quick and easy work. Those students will finish first and will be free to go. Students who haven't prepared, who've got an incomplete or messy draft, if held to the same standards may need the entire class time to write this outline (and possibly still not be done). So not only is the well-prepared student "rewarded," the unprepared students are "punished."

Of course, this "punishment" is not really a punishment at all—it allows you to give them the individual attention they need, and the more time you spend with these students as they navigate their way through the writing process, the more they will learn, the better their papers will be, the easier your job becomes, the better your life becomes, and so on and so forth. If these students do see having to stay for the full time while others are set free as a sort of "punishment," they will be motivated to work harder in the future to avoid being punished again. So if you follow Sun Tzu's advice on both reward and discipline, your students will trust you, listen to you, and maybe even appreciate you when all is said and done. But even if that is not the case, the way you use these tools should make your students better writers and make your job teaching them easier.

Dealing With Enemies

Since we are discussing warfare, there must be enemies, right? Yes, and I've already talked about the first kind of enemy, which is simply Bad Writing (bad writing habits, laziness, a lack of appreciation for language, et cetera). You can also view much of the communications favored by modern society as antagonistic to good writing; that is, communication best served by thoughtful writing now comes in the form of texts, tweets, sound bites, PowerPoints, photographs, and the like. Higher-level thinking (and I don't mean to sound elitist—I just mean the type of thinking that is the result of genuinely taking the time *to think*) simply isn't appreciated in many facets of life. Lots of people seem to feel it is possible to get by without it, and in some circles, there's a resistance to complexity. Look around and see how many simple ideas abound. For example, superficial lists are everywhere; every day there's a new Top Ten this or a Top Ten that—beaches, movies, books, body parts. To rank things is to simplify them, to use the clumsy, imprecise term of "better." The bigger problem is that it usually stops there, without inquiry and explanation. Every year *Esquire* tells us who the World's Sexiest Woman is. Meanwhile, *People* annually crowns the World's Sexiest Man. If there could be such things! But people believe what they are told. Simple comparisons also abound. Which is better? This great quarterback or that one? Hawaii or Bermuda? *War and Peace* or *Moby Dick*? While comparisons can be a helpful tool, and analogies are in fact a great way for writers to make points to readers in an interesting way, and I do have my students work on developing this skill, the Buddha was right when he said, "Comparisons are odious." By that he meant that sometimes we should simply consider what's at hand, appreciate the scenic road we are driving on instead of comparing it to other scenic roads, enjoy the chicken wings we are eating instead of comparing them to the wings from Hooters. If we focus on one thing, we can go further thinking about it. But people don't seem to want to put forth the effort to do this.

All right, let's get back to enemies in the composition class. I don't think anyone dreams of having enemies, but let's face it, sometimes they can provide energy and focus. Obviously, soldiers in battle must think: "It's me or the enemy." And in other less serious endeavors, there is still nothing like a rival to motivate one to reach new heights. For example, when Roger Bannister was trying to break four minutes for the mile, his determination and focus was fueled to a large extent by the fact that at the same time, fellow runners John Landy and Wes Santee were also getting close to doing the same thing. If they hadn't been, Bannister surely wouldn't have worked so hard. He could have put things off, given himself more time. He was also in medical school at the time and had other things to do.

But he knew if he didn't break four minutes soon, someone else would beat him to it.

Sometimes as a teacher, I like to imagine an adversary—someone who doesn't care about writing at all, a real skeptic who doesn't care about thinking, self-actualization, humanity—who says we're all just superficial, caught up in the machine, doomed to a life of fuzzy mediocrity, someone who believes it's not at all important to have clear, thorough, and organized thoughts. This adversary is someone who not only doesn't believe in The Way, but believes in the opposite, the Wrong Way. Sometimes I imagine my students spend time with this person regularly, that this enemy is teaching them as well, for the twenty-three hours of the day they're not in class. "And my foe is persuasive," I tell myself, "alluring, this devil of The Wrong Way." This gives me a nice sense of urgency, helps keep me focused. I like to imagine my students going back to this person throughout the semester and first being skeptical, then questioning, then resistant, and finally renouncing this false prophet altogether.

But enough about imaginary enemies, because you will have some real ones in class: students who don't yet believe in The Way, who see "another writing class" and every assignment as wastes of time. There will be others who think it doesn't matter for their majors, others who come to class on the first day ready to dismiss everything you say just out of spite, those who think they know it all already. Sadly, these students do exist and will fight you as long as they can in one form or another. Why do they come to the classroom with their metaphorical fists up?

There are a number of possibilities: they may have had bad teachers that soured them on writing, they may have inner demons (fear of failure, a history of failure, fear of success), they may have had gaps in their education or learning issues which have led to frustration (if this is the case, you'll want to get some help), or they may be resistant for lots of other reasons.

But whatever the reason some students are adversarial, your goal is always, through a variety of ingenious, covert techniques, to bring them into the fold, onto your team. But let's not get ahead of ourselves. Because once you've identified these enemies (again, I am now defining enemies as those who are not simply indifferent, but genuinely opposed to you or the class), you need to treat them as such, which means be careful, cautious, and diligent. They have the potential to make trouble for you and their classmates.

So, how do we deal with these "enemies"? First, Sun Tzu says (in reference to opposition), "In warfare...keeping a squad intact is best, destroying a squad, second best." This means you need to keep your enemies "intact" because they will become your soldiers eventually, leaving the class at the end of the semester stronger writers, with a newfound appreciation for writing and thinking. But how does one deal with these enemies? Well, there's no formula, but the first thing you'll need to do is identify them. This should be rather easy over the first few weeks of the semester, seeing their writing, their thoughts on writing, how they act in class, having an initial conference, getting to know them. You'll be getting to know all your students in the same way, and these folks are usually easy enough to spot.

Sun Tzu also says, "One who knows when he can fight, and when he cannot fight, will be victorious." This means once you have identified them, what you don't want to do is attack too soon, even though you know you are so right and they are so wrong. The "when" in this quote is critical because timing in teaching is important and the key is to know when to engage the students directly and when to wait.

He also says, "If they are strong, avoid them." Early in the semester, they'll be strong, primarily in their convictions: that writing and the class are a waste of time, or worse, that you are a buffoon, or eccentric, or out of touch with reality. At this point, it's best to study them, but from a distance, and this is the meaning of "avoidance." Combative students should have no idea you are taking special notice of them. This way they'll get comfortable, let their guards down. If you come on too aggressively at the beginning of the semester, they'll just brace themselves for the duration—like they're about to take a hit, thinking: "I've just got to protect myself and get through this. I won't let it get to me. I won't let it."

When you avoid these "enemies," it results in them marinating in their doubts or skepticism or anger as the other students in the class show signs of life and begin to build momentum. If they see others doing well and not suffering, resistant students, though they might not "get it" right away, will lower their resistance. Then you can start to work on them. Some of your enemies might come off as loners, they might isolate themselves, but no matter how aloof they act, they don't want to stay that way. It's human nature not to. Remember Maslow's Hierarchy of Needs—nobody wants to be alone.

Sun Tzu says you've got to get them to come to you. Students might exhibit behaviors that seem to be adversarial, but these might be bluffs. Or you might win them over right way with the way you turn a phrase, read an excerpt, hand out an assignment sheet, or write notes on the board. The principles discussed earlier for "luring students to the battle-field" also apply to enemies, but they will be more resistant. The key is to get them to the place where they'll engage with you (in whatever form that takes) and open their minds to thinking about writing in a new way.

I think it's important to get all your students to think about writing—what it is, why it matters. But it's even more important for those most resistant to it. If a student starts the semester thinking about writing in the wrong way, at least you've got something to work with. You can start a dialogue that gets them thinking about writing and take it from there. If a student seems really determined to *not* get invested in the class, you could ask for a paper explaining why writing doesn't matter—an impossible task because completing it successfully disproves the argument. Or if students think they are too good for the class, already great writers, well, it's easy enough to show them how to improve. There is no such thing as a perfect writer. You can teach your students that, along with humility.

Sun Tzu says, "Getting the enemy to approach on his own accord is a matter of showing him advantage." That is why it is sometimes important to let your resistant students write about what is important to them in their heart-of-hearts, whether it is swimming, veganism, the NRA, or the NBA. Let these students "show off" what they know. This allows them to "show advantage" and feel like they are in control. But once these thoughts and ideas have been put into words and submitted to you, they are entering your territory. To try to maintain their advantage, which they will want to do, they'll need to develop their ideas, clarify, reorganize, explain. They'll need to write about them. In a lot of ways, dealing with enemies is the same as dealing with the rest of your students, only harder.

Regarding enemies, Sun Tzu also says, "The best warfare is to attack the enemy's plans, next is to attack alliances, next is to attack the army, and the worst is to attack a walled city." Let's start with the worst, or what *not* to do. Why don't you attack a "walled city"? Because you're not going to get inside, and you're going to hurt yourself trying. What do I mean by a walled city? Well, I've explained why it's bad to attack the person—that student will get into a defensive position and stay there for the whole semester, no matter what else you do. In this same vein, you don't want to try to convince someone there is or isn't a God or that the Democrats (or Republicans, or Libertarians) are best for the country. People's opinions on topics like these are often held safely behind walls so thick and tall they can't be overcome through something as simple as an attack.

Sun Tzu also says don't attack "the army." What this means is don't attack the whole class. Never throw up your hands and say (literally or otherwise), "This class just doesn't get it. This class can't write!" Writing classes, more than others it seems, take on their own personalities no matter what you do. Earlier, I said you want to unite the class, and attacking the class is one way to do that, but if attacked, they'll not just see themselves as a group, they'll band together, tighten their formation, and shut you out.

It may seem that I'm stating the obvious here: you wouldn't "attack" your students. And though it's true you may not verbalize this, you can communicate it in other subtler ways too and do just as much damage, dismissing whole groups of people, perhaps without even realizing you are doing it. The key is having the right attitude I talked about earlier, so your natural, spontaneous expression conveys to all your students that you *do* care about their success and that you *do* believe they can succeed, all of them.

If you know this is not true, if you've been through this process enough times to know that at the end of the semester there will be some bodies left behind, students that fail to do the work in one way or another, you need to convince yourself to believe otherwise. Enter into a sort of fiction, like when you are reading a novel, and suspend disbelief, at least until the end of the semester. They can all succeed! The result: you'll feel better all the way through knowing there are no lost causes. You'll teach everyone in the class better. And you will be more likely to bring enemies over to your side.

Sun Tzu says it's good to break up alliances, and this is relevant for our purposes. Alliances can be groups of like-minded students: friends, teammates on sports teams, et cetera. If they've got a plan to "get by" without doing the work, they'll do it. Students can be very resourceful when they want to get out of something. Sometimes students will form a subset inside the class—a group of co-conspirators aiming to defeat you, or at least make the class easy, or not let you affect them in any way. You don't want to attack these groups either; they will only cling tighter to each other, form a stronger "walled city."

Sun Tzu's advice for effectively attacking enemies is to "attack their plans." In composition class, the enemy's plans will be to: take shortcuts, be lazy, turn in first drafts for grades, turn in old papers for grades, not challenge themselves, not learn and grow. You simply can't let them do this. The assignment sequence for the class should include multiple readings, multiple drafts of essays, outlines, reflections, et cetera. If you require your students to go through all the stages of the process an experienced writer employs as a matter of necessity, any ill-conceived plans they may have had will be difficult, if not impossible, for them to follow.

Sun Tzu says, "If they are united, separate them." Of course, over the course of the semester, you will have lots of opportunities to "separate them"—when they do their own writing, when you write comments on their drafts, when you meet with them for individual conferences. Sometimes students may act one way in class, but are altogether different in one-on-one dialogue. That's why it is important to schedule a conference early in the semester, to help you see who you are dealing with.

But peer pressure is strong, so you may find that the earnest, engaged student you met with in an individual conference falls right back into his or her group mode in the classroom, whether it is self-defeating, disruptive, apathetic, or something else. Giving more individual exercises is an easy solution, but you don't want to lose the advantage you gain by using groups, so that means you need to break up problematic groups. The key is to not make it appear you are singling anyone out. If you want to separate groups, you need to mix up all of them, even the ones that have proven to be engaged and productive. You don't necessarily have to put the resistant (or weaker) students in groups with the strongest ones—this often puts them on the defensive. Sometimes it works to put resistant students in groups with other resistant students they don't typically work with. The simple change in scenery can help get them more engaged. Sometimes it's better chemistry that helps. Try different combinations. There is no secret prescription. Observe them the best you can and make your best decisions based on what you observe. You will likely want to arrive in class with these decisions made. Don't try to assess and form new groups in front of students.

Sun Tzu's advice to "separate them" also serves as good advice if your whole class is not as engaged with the material as you need them to be. For example, if you are having a whole-class discussion on a problematic draft and they all say, "Looks good," choosing not to engage, split them up into groups to argue for and against that claim, some students focusing on the draft's strengths, doing all they can to say it *is* meeting the assignment goals, and having others focus on the weaknesses, all the ways it *is not* meeting assignment goals and/or succeeding as a piece of writing. You can even make it a contest—see which side can come up with more valid points. Ultimately, both sides should reach the same conclusion—that the draft has got problems.

Sun Tzu says, "A defeated army first seeks to do battle, then obtains conditions for victory." While you don't want to make assignments easy, you want to make following all the proper steps of the process ultimately *easier* than what they may otherwise do. If it's easier to do the work as directed than it is to take shortcuts or even cheat, they will likely follow the directions. Once they figure this out, they will do what you want them to do. And focusing on process and drafting as part of your assignment sequence helps prevent plagiarism because you'll see works grow one step at a time. If a student turns in something completely new when it's time for a grade, something that hasn't evolved over the course of the semester, you should be suspicious. If a student hasn't written clearly and eloquently about his or her own experiences earlier in the semester, you shouldn't expect him or her to improve drastically when writing about more challenging, academic topics later (I mean, you're a good teacher, but you're probably not that good). Yes, it's hard to imagine that one of your students, whom you have worked with for months, would try to pull this over on you. It's easy to think, "Well, I never knew John, a mediocre student all semester, had such enthusiasm and could write so well on Germline Gene Therapy, a topic we have never even discussed in class." Sadly, this happens, which I guess goes to show that some enemies can't be helped. My advice here is to send this student a clear message, a grade of "zero" for the assignment, or an F for the class, maybe let him or her write another paper to make up for it. This all depends on your department and university policies and what you have learned about the student over the course of the semester. But in a case like this, you may just have to let this student go. Some are not yet ready for instruction in The Way. Hopefully when this student is ready to learn, as the saying goes, a new teacher will appear. But this is the exception. Most enemies *can* be helped.

What else can you do to win over these enemies? Sun Tzu says, "If you surround the enemy, leave an outlet." This means don't make your enemies too desperate—they will just get scared and fight harder, make worse decisions, burn bridges. Always leave a path for retreat. Since your goal is to bring the enemy to your side, always leave a path that leads right to your team. Always give your enemies the option of coming over to your side.

One mistake I see some teachers make is seeing enemies where there are none. That's why it is important in the first few weeks of the semester as you're paying attention, probing your students so stealthily they don't even realize it, watching for potential enemies, that you don't jump to any conclusions. For example, if your students believe in God, guns, and taxes in ways you don't, for the purposes of the class at least, they are not your enemies. Remember that your job is to teach them to write, not change their views of the world. Now while this may seem to contradict what I've already said about enlightening them, showing them The Way, it's best to work *around* any entrenched thoughts, ideas, philosophies, and habits unrelated to writing, no matter how strongly you may disagree with them. Sometimes that is hard to do, but rest assured, these will work themselves out over time after students have gained access to The Way. It may not happen in the semester you are teaching the student, and it may not ever happen to the extent that you desire, but if you teach someone to think things through, really think critically about a topic, if you are right about it, the inevitable result is that this other person will eventually come to the same conclusions as you. But your job is not to change anyone's mind on beliefs such as these.

Can these enemies defeat you? Yes, but only if you let them: if you let them frustrate you, if they convince you to give up on them, or if they still see you or writing as the enemy at the end of the semester. But you're not going to let that happen, are you? If you do, you're not doing your job, and even if you don't care about your students' welfare (though I know you do), you surely care about doing your job well. I mean, if you wanted to destroy some of your students, it would be so easy—just tell them what they are doing is wrong, that they are not good enough, that their writing stinks, keep pointing to all their mistakes. Say this and they'll believe it, and their fate will be sealed: no chance of succeeding in the class, no chance of becoming better writers, no chance of spreading the word of The Way to others, no chance of making the world a better place.

As Sun Tzu describes it, you should "replace the enemy's flags and standards with your own. Mix the captured chariots with your own, treat the captured soldiers well." By the end of the semester, or hopefully long before that, you will have brought all enemies over to your side, the side of The Way.

Final Thoughts

Well, I hope you have enjoyed my thoughts on using Sun Tzu's principles to improve your teaching. I'm not going to write a long conclusion because I know you are excited to get to work on your classes, get to work on improving the world! But before I let you go, I've got a few parting words.

First, how do you know if you have done a good job? Well, one way is by looking at the work they turn in. Is it better than the work they turned in at the beginning of the semester? If so, that's progress. But it's not that simple because, in addition to writing better, your students should also be able to see and understand the difference in the quality of their work. That is, it can't just be a matter of *you* seeing it has improved—*they* need to see that it has improved, and how, and why. If they can't, they haven't learned enough. This is why some kind of end-of-semester reflective writing is valuable, not only for students, but for you. And of course, if they write their reflective essays and talk about how much they learned and what a great class it was and what a great teacher you are, well, don't believe it. At least don't take it at face value. They are still writing for a grade. But if you look at their reflective writing along with everything else, well, then you should be able to get a pretty good view of what has happened over the course of the semester.

Secondly, what do you do with your failures, the students who still don't get it, or don't care, or can't write, despite your best intentions? Along with your successes, you have to take responsibility for these. Whatever happens, you can't blame them. If you do that, you are abdicating your responsibility, and even if there are students that could be categorized as "unreachable" or "unteachable" or maybe still in very formative stages of their writing lives, instead of dismissing them, you need to think about what you could have done differently, done better. If you dismiss your failures at the end of the semester as lost causes or archenemies, this will become a habit. You will walk into the classroom the next semester believing there are students who can't grow, and you'll make assumptions, and you'll surely make mistakes. Remember who you are and the task you've been given. Remember that your students are asking for your help and that your job is to do all you can to teach them. Trust me when I say that your students will surprise you, will succeed if you put them in positions to do so. Some will have more success than others, and very rarely do students fail completely. But if they do, find out why. Try not to let it happen again. Do a better job the next time. Just like a writer can always improve, so can a teacher. Even you.

It naturally follows that, just like your students, you will make mistakes. And just like your students, you can learn from them. To help yourself, keep a journal of your teaching—what happened in class? What worked and didn't work? Why? I don't do this as often as I should, which is one of my mistakes. But it's not the only one. I make mistakes every day. But I've found it's easier to accept my mistakes when I know I am doing my best. And on those days I am not doing my best, well, I know I need to be honest with myself and admit it, that I am shirking my responsibilities. I don't like this feeling and try to avoid it at all costs, though I suppose it is a never-ending battle. Even composition instructors are imperfect. Even me.

Every semester, I try to follow the principles I've laid out in this book, try to do my best for my students, to help them become better writers, students, people, but every semester, just after the final papers have been turned in, I get a feeling of dread, like I have surely failed, that I've missed opportunities, didn't work hard enough, was not clear enough, that I need more time. As glad as I am that the semester is over, and however much I am looking forward to the break ahead of me, I'm still always full of anxious regret, and I think to myself: "If I had another semester, another semester with these same students, I could do some real good!" Obviously, that would be better. A writing class every semester for four years would be better for students, but I wonder if even at the end of that I'd have the same feelings of not doing enough. I suppose this is just part of it because there's always more to teach, always more to learn. Regardless, as I said earlier, I always tell myself I will do better next time, and I always try to.

I wonder if Sun Tzu had these same misgivings. I mean, it was surely more clear to him if he had succeeded or not. A battle between armies has a more definitive, measurable outcome than a semester's worth of writing instruction.

But I'm sure he thought he could do better and he would lose soldiers along the way. What we are doing is not as important as that. Still, it is very important, and there's nothing I would rather do. Well, as long as I still have time left to spend with my family, take vacations, go for some good runs, read some books, do some writing of my own, watch the Packers play, et cetera, and so on. Those things are important too, but you know what I mean, right? Of course you do, you're a composition instructor, one of the blessed few. So I am going to stop trying to explain this or myself any further. You get it, right? You *get it*. Yes, you do. Thanks for reading, and now go get to work!

Acknowledgements

I would like to thank readers of early drafts of this book, who responded with enough enthusiasm to encourage me to keep working on it, specifically Kate Lorenz (xo), Frank Sikora, Holly Christianson, and Jeff Perso. I'd also like to thank Shannon Ishizaki and the whole team at Orange Hat Publishing/Ten16 Press. While working on this book, I was fortunate enough to enjoy a residency at the Rockvale Writers Colony (thanks, Sandy Coomer). Finally, I am deeply indebted to my editor Margaret Dwyer, whose expertise and guidance helped shape this book into its best version of itself.

List of Works Cited and/or Referred To

"A Forever Connection Love Card." *Hallmark US*, https://www.hallmark.com/cards/greeting-cards/a-forever-connection-love-card-429LOV1389.html.

Aristotle. "The Aim of Man." *The Internet Classics Archive | Nicomachean Ethics by Aristotle.* http://classics.mit.edu/Aristotle/nicomachaen.1.i.html.

Asch, Sholem. *Quotes about Writing.* http://pasikarppanen.net/quotes/q-writ.htm.

Baumeister, Roy F. "The Self and Society: Changes, Problems, and Opportunities." *Mind Readings*, Bedford/St. Martin's, 2001.

Bodhidharma. *Zen to Go: Bite-Sized Bits of Wisdom, Ed. John Winokur.* Sasquatch Books; Distributed by Publishers Group West, 2005.

Churchill, Winston. *Planning Quotes.* https://www.santabanta.com/sms/quotes/planning/664/.

Ciardi, John. "John Ciardi Quotes About Writing." *A-Z Quotes*, https://www.azquotes.com/author/2891-John_Ciardi/tag/writing.

Czikszenthihalyi, Mihaly. "What Is the Self?" *Mind Readings: An Anthology for Writers*, Bedford/St. Martin's, 2001.

Dass, Ram. *Zen to Go: Bite-Sized Bits of Wisdom, Ed. Jon Winokur.* Sasquatch Books; Distributed by Publishers Group West, 2005.

Derrida, Jacques, and Christie McDonald. *The Ear of the Other: Otobiography, Transference, Translation: Texts and Discussions with Jacques Derrida*. University of Nebraska Press, 1988.

Dickinson, Emily. "For Each Ecstatic Instant." *Dickinson, Emily Complete Poems*. https://www.bartleby.com/113/1037.html.

---. "I Had a Daily Bliss." *Dickinson, Emily Complete Poems*, https://www.bartleby.com/113/1120.html.

Didion, Joan. "Why I Write." *The New York Times*, 5 Dec. 1976. *NYTimes.com*, https://www.nytimes.com/1976/12/05/archives/why-i-write-why-i-write.html.

Dillard, Annie. "Living Like Weasels." *Teaching a Stone to Talk: Expeditions and Encounters*. Harper Perennial, 2013.

---. *The Writing Life*. Harper Perennial, 1995.

Elbow, Peter. *Peter Elbow: The Democratization of Writing*. http://peterelbow.com/index.html.

Emerson, Ralph Waldo. "Self-Reliance: Change Your Life For The Better." *Ralph Waldo Emerson*, https://emersoncentral.com/texts/essays-first-series/self-reliance/.

Engel, Susan. "Then and Now: Creating a Self Through the Past." *Mind Readings*, Bedford/St. Martin's, 2001.

Forster, E.M. "E. M. Forster Quotes About Writing." *A-Z Quotes*, https://www.azquotes.com/author/5018-E_M_Forster/tag/writing.

Frankl, Viktor E. *Man's Search for Meaning*. Beacon Press, 2006.

Hemingway, Ernest. "9 Insightful Quotes on the Process of Writing." *Super Copy Editors*, https://supercopyeditors.com/blog/writing/quotes-about-the-process-of-writing/.

Herrigel, Eugen. *Zen in the Art of Archery*. Vintage Books, 1999.

Hesse, Hermann. *Siddhartha*. Translated by Hilda Rosner, Bantam Books, 1971.

Huynh, Thomas. *The Art of War—Spirituality for Conflict: Annotated & Explained*. SkyLight Paths Pub, 2008.

Greene, Robert. *Robert Greene - Being Self-Reliant. www.youtube.com*, https://www.youtube.com/watch?v=8zf3ve2az58.

Johnson, Brian. *PNTV: Self-Reliance by Ralph Waldo Emerson (#378). www.youtube.com*. https://www.youtube.com/watch?v=PwoGpCd4DQE.

Johnson, Samuel. *The Importance of Editing and Proof-Reading | SlawTips*. https://tips.slaw.ca/2016/research/the-importance-of-editing-and-proof-reading/.

Joy, Amy. "9 Insightful Quotes on the Process of Writing." *Super Copy Editors*, https://supercopyeditors.com/blog/writing/quotes-about-the-process-of-writing/.

Kerouac, Jack. *The Dharma Bums*. Penguin Books, 2006.

King, Jr, Martin Luther. "Letter from a Birmingham Jail." *The Martin Luther King, Jr, Research and Education Institute*, Stanford University, https://kinginstitute.stanford.edu/encyclopedia/letter-birmingham-jail.

Krakauer, Jon. *Into Thin Air: A Personal Account of the Mount Everest Disaster*. Anchor Books, 1999.

Laabs, Jeremiah. "Jeremiah Laabs Quotes." *Best Quotes Ever*, https://www.bestquotes4ever.com/authors/jeremiah-laabs-quotes.

Lee, Bruce. "Bruce Lee Quotes." *BrainyQuote*, https://www.brainyquote.com/authors/bruce-lee-quotes.

Lee, Stan. https://www.goodreads.com/quotes/235999-with-great-power-comes-great-responsibility.

Machiavelli, Nicolo. *The Project Gutenberg EBook of The Prince, by Nicolo Machiavelli*. https://www.gutenberg.org/files/1232/1232-h/1232-h.htm.

Malaquais, Jean. https://quotefancy.com/quote/1589706/Jean-Malaquais.

Mann, Thomas. "Quotes about the Difficulty of Writing." *Wylie Communications, Inc.*, https://www.wyliecomm. com/writing-tips/processes-for-writing-and-communication/writing-process/quotes-on-the-difficulty-of-writing/.

Mcleod, Saul. "Maslow's Hierarchy of Needs." *Simply Psychology*, 29 Dec. 2020, https://www.simplypsychology.org/maslow.html.

McNeilly, Mark. *Sun Tzu and the Art of Business: Six Strategic Principles for Managers*. Rev. ed, Oxford University Press, 2012.

Neruda, Pablo. "XVII (I do not love you...)." *Hello Poetry*, https://hellopoetry.com/poem/9959/xvii-i-do-not-love-you/.

Nietzsche, Friedrich. "Morality as Anti-Nature." *Nietzsche: Twilight of the Idols*. http://www.handprint.com/SC/NIE/GotDamer.html#sect5.

Pauling, Linus. "Writing and the Creative Life: 'The Best Way to Have a Good Idea...' by Scott Myers." *Medium*, 22 June 2018, https://gointothestory.blcklst.com/writing-and-the-creative-life-the-best-way-to-have-a-good-idea-e74d5c14cf0a.

Plato. *The Allegory of the Cave*. https://scholar.harvard.edu/files/seyer/files/plato_republic_514b-518d_allegory-of-the-cave.pdf.

Platt, Norbert. "World's Best Norbert Platt Quotes Images to Share and Download." *Quoteslyfe*, https://www.quoteslyfe.com/author/Norbet-Platt-quotes.

Quenqua, Douglas. "Seeing Narcissists Everywhere." *The New York Times*, 5 Aug. 2013. *NYTimes.com*, https://www.nytimes.com/2013/08/06/science/seeing-narcissists-everywhere.html.

Rogell, Eric. *The Art of War for Dating*. Adams Media, 2011.

Russell, Bertrand. "The Happy Life Bertrand Russell | Virtue | Bertrand Russell." *Scribd*, https://www.scribd.com/document/339718817/The-Happy-Life-Bertrand-Russell.

Sheetz-Runkle, Becky. *Sun Tzu for Women: The Art of War for Winning in Business*. Adams Media, 2011.

Singer, Isaac Bashavis. *Great Quotes about Writing | Killzoneblog. Com*. https://killzoneblog.com/2014/12/great-quotes-about-writing.html.

Stafford, William. *A Way of Writing*. http://williamglewis.pbworks.com/w/file/fetch/84886471/Essay1Stafford.pdf.

Turkle, Sherry. "Opinion | Stop Googling. Let's Talk." *The New York Times*, 26 Sept. 2015. *NYTimes.com*, https://www.nytimes.com/2015/09/27/opinion/sunday/stop-googling-lets-talk.html.

Walter, Benjamin. "Top 30 Quotes of WALTER BENJAMIN" *Inspiring Quotes*, https://www.inspiringquotes.us/author/1740-walter-benjamin.

Zinsser, William. "Top 30 Quotes of WILLIAM ZINSSER." *Inspiring Quotes*, https://www.inspiringquotes.us/author/2277-william-zinsser.

Steven T. Nelson has been teaching college-level writing classes for over 25 years. He earned his PhD in Creative Writing from the University of Wisconsin-Milwaukee and has had works of fiction and nonfiction published in various literary journals. He contributed to the short story anthology *Our Plan to Save the World* and is a Professor of English at Concordia University Wisconsin.

For more on Steven T. Nelson and his work, please visit: ***teaching-the-way.com***